Twentieth-Century
Textbook Wars

HISTORY OF SCHOOLS & SCHOOLING

Alan R. Sadovnik and Susan F. Semel
General Editors

Vol. 17

PETER LANG
New York • Washington, D.C./Baltimore • Bern
Frankfurt am Main • Berlin • Brussels • Vienna • Oxford

Gerard Giordano

Twentieth-Century Textbook Wars

A History of Advocacy and Opposition

PETER LANG
New York • Washington, D.C./Baltimore • Bern
Frankfurt am Main • Berlin • Brussels • Vienna • Oxford

Library of Congress Cataloging-in-Publication Data

Giordano, Gerard.
Twentieth-century textbook wars:
a history of advocacy and opposition / Gerard Giordano.
p. cm. — (History of schools and schooling; vol. 17)
Includes bibliographical references and index.
1. Textbooks—United States—History—20th century. 2. Textbooks—Publishing—
United States—History—20th century. 3. Textbook bias—United States—History—
20th century. I. Title. II. History of schools and schooling; v. 17.
LB3047 .G56   379.1'56'09730904—dc21   00-062952
ISBN 0-8204-5228-9
ISSN 1089-0678

Die Deutsche Bibliothek-CIP-Einheitsaufnahme

Giordano, Gerard:
Twentieth-century textbook wars:
a history of advocacy and opposition / Gerard Giordano.
–New York; Washington, D.C./Baltimore; Bern;
Frankfurt am Main; Berlin; Brussels; Vienna; Oxford: Lang.
(History of schools and schooling; Vol. 17)
ISBN 0-8204-5228-9

Cover design by Joni Holst

The paper in this book meets the guidelines for permanence and durability
of the Committee on Production Guidelines for Book Longevity
of the Council of Library Resources.

© 2003 Peter Lang Publishing, Inc., New York
275 Seventh Avenue, 28th Floor, New York, NY 10001
www.peterlangusa.com

Printed in the United States of America

For Gabe, Kara, and Peter,

Who have brought

So much joy into my life.

ACKNOWLEDGMENTS

I am so grateful to Amy Wilberg, Rebecca Cowley, Martha Hyder, and Bill Morgan for their diligence and resourcefulness in helping me complete the research for this book. Amy and Rebecca also demonstrated great professionalism and inexhaustible patience while preparing the final copy of the manuscript.

TABLE OF CONTENTS

ILLUSTRATIONS

TABLES

PREFACE

"The most dogged pursuers of agony are the critics of textbooks, those steadfast readers of readers, of classroom anthologies and of histories authored by committees." (Schrag, 1967)

Though the entire educational system was besieged throughout the 1900s, textbooks were singled out for unusually ferocious strikes. In a professional text about problems in American schools, McCullough (1922) indicated the importance of this topic by assigning six of 13 chapters to textbooks. He explicitly stated that "the school book question has been and is the most mischievous unsettled educational question before the people today" (p. 234). He left no doubt in his readers' minds about the length of this debate when he recapitulated a litany of textbook accusations that had begun in the 1830s.

Most educators ignored these accusations. Even after prices had escalated dramatically, textbooks remained highly regarded and ubiquitous. Surveys confirmed that parents and educators saw textbooks as essential classroom tools. Even strident critics admitted that extensive use validated the public's confidence in textbooks. Widespread at the beginning of the century, this use grew uninterruptedly throughout subsequent decades. Why were textbooks so popular? Why were they attacked so aggressively? Why weren't the attacks more successful?

Much of the initial criticism had concerned finances. Though early nineteenth-century schools had insisted that families supply their children's books, the schools of the late 1800s began to require uniform learning materials. To enforce this requirement, districts purchased textbooks and then distributed them free to students. Ambitious publishers were accused of exploiting the districts that became dependent on them. As an antidote, California and Kansas required adoption of textbooks published by their states. Opponents of state published textbooks protested that a competitive market ensured that the finest school materials were available. They predicted that the California and Kansas initiatives would fail because of higher than anticipated expenses, inadequate supplies of books, and the deficient quality of the materials. Critics of the textbook industry lost a good portion of their credibility after all of these predictions turned out to be correct.

In addition to being linked to greed and corruption, textbook publishers were vilified for transforming once lackluster materials through extensive illustrations, novel learning features, and high interest vignettes. Critics renounced this new generation of classroom materials for depleting teachers' instructional creativity. Textbook advocates retorted that schools needed to depend on textbooks because they were the best guarantee of quality education. Although they did acknowledge that some experienced instructors had relied excessively on their materials, textbook defenders thought this problem originated with teachers rather than the materials themselves.

Finance and pedagogy were the two fronts on which early attacks had been made made. When they saw that parents and educators were unresponsive, textbook opponents chose a distinct tact, charging that the materials were out of synchrony with changing societal values. Recognizing the potency of these accusations, publishers indicated that they were willing to make adaptations. However, they had to determine to which social critics they should be attentive. For example, early twentieth-century political liberals had railed at schoolbooks for developing an incendiary strain of patriotism. Conservatives were equally fervent, but for the opposite reason. They feared that inordinately pacifist textbooks were undermining national security. During World War I, World War II, and the periods that immediately followed, most publishers enhanced the nationalist content within their textbooks. Although political liberals did convince a few publishers to promote international cooperation during World War II, the campaigns to suppress nationalistic textbooks were more successful during eras marked by domestic discord. For example, politically liberal ideologies were apparent in the textbooks produced during the 1930s Depression and then later during the Vietnam War protests.

After textbook publishers began to excise religious content, critics cited this as another issue on which school materials were out of synchrony with societal values. Even though they found these omissions disconcerting, the critics were even more concerned about schoolbooks that actually undermined their fundamental religious beliefs. The most publicized example was the 1920s "Scopes Monkey Trial" that permanently stirred up emotions about the interrelation of science, theology, and the schools. In response, textbook publishers made adaptations. To emphasize that controversial scientific information was speculative, some of them replaced references to *evidence of evolution* with phrases about the *theory of evolution*. Others completely deleted the term *evolution* and substituted less volatile synonyms. Though textbook opponents rejected those adaptations with which they disagreed, they even denigrated some of the changes with which they were in philosophical accord when they viewed these as token alterations.

Though 1960s critics were still concerned about nationalistic and religious biases, they concentrated more intently on racial bias. The national movement to affirm civil rights prodded questions about why racial minority groups appeared so infrequently in the illustrations and text of instructional materials. Similar to the changes they had made in response to previous social movements, some textbook publishers made expedient alterations. However, many of these alterations were as superficial as they were swift. One publisher created new editions by merely darkening the faces of the nonminority children in photographs. Another publisher produced "multiethnic" and "standard" editions for markets with different racial profiles.

Because publishers did significantly reduce racial textbook bias before the end of the 1960s, proponents of the 1970s Women's Rights Movement demanded that gender bias be expurgated with the same aggressiveness. Publishers reacted by increasing the illustrations of females, textual references to females, and portrayals of women in leadership activities. Publishers also replaced terms such as *men* when gender-neutral terms such as *persons* or *people* could be used.

Although many critics were concerned primarily about the broad educational system, textbooks may have been targeted because they were pervasive symbols of that larger system and because their accessibility seemed to ensure an easy conquest. Textbooks were initially attacked for being products of businesspersons whose financial interests could conflict with sound education. However, these charges became inconsequential after critics were unable to establish an alternative model for producing textbooks. Textbooks were then blamed for undermining teacher creativity. More worried about student learning, most persons ignored this accusation and continued to view textbooks as indispensable to sound curricula.

Critics also struck at textbooks for being out of step with changing social values. Though these accusations could have been damaging, the analytical documentation used in the attacks actually helped publishers. For clearly defined faults were eliminated through precise adaptations. As a consequence, publishers were able to turn away assaults from enraged critics while they simultaneously bolstered their rapport with clients.

Publishers also strengthened their bond to the public by capitalizing on another liability, their delay in making textbook adaptations. Though some of their caution resulted from genuine confusion about complex social issues, deliberative publishers were railed at for being cowardly, profit-centered, and unethical. Irrespective of its origin, this concern about the timing for implementing changes required publishers to focus on their clients' attitudes. This acute attention to the public contributed to an impregnable defense beyond which the hostile critics of twentieth-century textbooks were unable to penetrate.

CHAPTER ONE

Textbooks as Products—
The Business Era

The nineteenth-century textbook market grew robustly after schools began to distribute free books to students. Publishers initially used the revenues from the additional sales to contain production expenses. However, as the true cost of publishing rose, prices escalated correspondingly. Some critics castigated publishers for making excessive profits and disguising these with inflated statements of expenses. Reports about ruthless salesmen increased speculations about publishers' questionable ethics. In response, state legislators threatened to restrict textbook purchases to materials that had been published by the state. Even so, many persons were skeptical about the quality and real costs of state-published textbooks. In the end, only California and Kansas actually implemented these restrictions. Although criticism about excessive expenses never abated, the publishing market remained strong. However, the increasing amount of money needed to design, produce, and market books eventually did lead to a reduced number of textbook firms.

Conflict of Interest

Even before the twentieth century, critics had pointed to the conflicting interests of publishers who wished to simultaneously make effective materials and high profits. Jenks (1906) reported about the political turmoil after an 1889 legislative committee discovered that more than 75 percent of Indiana's textbooks had been purchased from a single firm. Similar to many of his contemporaries, Jenks was not prepared to condemn the publishers. His ambivalence toward the incriminating evidence was apparent in the tortured logic he employed to dismiss their culpability.

> But though the methods employed by agents may at times have been doubtful, and though the publishers may not always have inquired too curiously into the means employed by their agents in making sales, it is not to be believed that the methods of school-book men were more corrupt than those ordinarily employed by other wholesale dealers who have to do with public functionaries. Nor can one who has been acquainted with hundreds of school teachers believe that the teachers and trustees of a state as a whole were purchased by one or by several book firms. But this much at least may safely be asserted, that the means employed by publishers to urge books upon the schools have not always been fair, and that it is not surprising that

efforts have been made to check them, though these efforts may not always have been wisely directed. (Jenks, 1906, p. 221)

Fitzpatrick (1912) acknowledged potential ethical conflicts when he wrote that a textbook salesperson "exists directly to point out and exploit the aims and methods of the author of the textbook that he is trying to sell" and only "indirectly, to help the schools" (p. 284). Nevertheless, he was still sure that only narrow-minded persons would regard book agents as evil and reasoned that the best textbooks would be produced only through commercial and educational cooperation. Two years earlier, Ginn (1910), the head of one of the largest textbook publishing firms, had also defended textbook agents. He wrote that most of these agents were preeminently well-qualified college graduates who only "occasionally, in their zeal to secure business" made transactions that were "of less benefit to the public than to the publisher" (p. 224).

Not all advocates of textbooks were willing to concede that publishing produced inevitable conflicts between schools and book companies. For example, Armstrong (1911) confronted those critics who thought that textbook publishers had surrendered their ethics to pursue huge profits. He wrote that the average annual cost of all California texts for each student was $1.13, significantly less than most citizens had conjectured. Although he cited this statistic to convince his readers that textbooks were priced reasonably, Armstrong's figure may have actually been higher than the average for most other parts of the country. For example, Hilton (1913) cited figures from a 1911 report of the U.S. Commissioner of Education that indicated the average annual cost of textbooks at less than 70 cents per pupil. Another report ("Kansas Decision," 1913) estimated the average annual textbook cost in Michigan at 55 cents per pupil.

Chancellor (1913) established four motives for publishing textbooks. The initial three were to enable firms to make payments to stockholders, employees, and authors. Though some publishers paid authors high royalties, he argued that they did this to recruit talented individuals who could create the best books. Chancellor then pointed to a fourth incentive for publishing, which was creating superior books at a reasonable cost. He disagreed with those who claimed that large publishing houses owned the markets for entire cities or states and thought this impression might have been formed because some textbook agents were simply shrewd judges of character who had adroitly identified school personnel who could help them in their business.

One editorialist ("Economizing in Text-books," 1918) admitted that textbooks were sometimes retired early from school districts because of a fear by the administrators that they would not appear progressive. Although the writer thought that publishers had deliberately encouraged such insecurity, he identified appropriate reasons for changing textbooks frequently, one of which was that new textbooks "make a break in the weary routine of teaching" and that "even if they are not better, it is something to have them different" (p. 294). Maxwell (1921) also reported that public distrust was aroused when schools changed textbooks frequently. In fact, he judged that the graft associated with textbook selection had brought more hostile criticism upon educators than any other scandal. Although he acknowledged the corruption, he thought that the "petty politicians" who were elected to school boards had been primarily responsible. He concluded that newer, systematized methods for selecting textbooks had eliminated the opportunities for unscrupulous textbook agents.

Douglas (1924) was another proponent of textbooks who conceded that publishers were in business to make money, but he was convinced that they did this by providing quality products. He observed that American publishing companies had hired specialized editors to ensure that the most promising manuscripts were identified and developed. Not only did he respect the editors, but Douglas thought that even the salespersons had professional experiences that complemented their commercial training. He judged that the competitive foundation, the basis for American textbook publishing, had simultaneously kept prices down and raised quality. With a similar appreciation for the critical role of capitalism, Thomas (1924) wrote that publishing enterprises should be patterned after those in the automobile industry, where quality of products rather than the personalities of sales agents determined profits. Table 1.1 (p. 4) contains early twentieth-century quotations about textbooks as products. A good portion of these quotes refers to the consternation created by the dual identity of firms in which personnel developed and sold educational materials.

Markets Created by Free Textbooks

Textbooks became more profitable because of the expanded market that resulted from their free distribution in the schools. The distribution of free textbooks developed from a prior initiative to ensure that schooling itself was free to all children. The free school movement had become progressively visible in the late nineteenth century. At an address to the National Educational Association, Tash (1888) judged that a national consensus supporting free schools had been formed. However, he argued that free schools would

Table 1.1   Early Twentieth-Century Criticism of Textbooks as Products

"The [California] State printer...expressed the opinion that a text-book similar to Monteith's Comprehensive geography, the retail price of which was $1.50, could be published for thirty-five cents." (Faulkner, 1900)

"Much capital and business enterprise go into the making of text-books." (Dutton & Snedden, 1909)

"The first objection raised against the plan of uniform textbooks is that it breeds graft." (Crissey, 1912)

"If the number of school books sold and the profits upon them were as gigantic as these cheap politicians and self-appointed guardians of the helpless public misrepresent them to be, the great money kings of Wall Street would abandon that little New York alley, waylay the publishers some dark night, wrench the business from them, and then retire to their palaces to dream of other Utopian fields of sufficient magnitude in which the profits might be invested." ("Facts About School," 1913)

"Ten years of bad editing would ruin any publishing house in America; and five years of great editing would put almost any house of good business methods in the millionaire class." (Chancellor, 1913)

"It is a popular cry [about textbook publishers] that we are in the hands of a great octopus that is squeezing the life out of us." (Evans, 1914)

"The great improvement that has been made in text-books is the result of competition among publishers." (State Superintendent of Kansas, quoted by McCray, 1914)

"Our system of textbook making is not only the greatest in the world, but it is very nearly the greatest feature in American education." (Winship, 1915, quoted by Jensen, 1931)

"[When purchasing instructional materials,] do not rely on the claims of text-book agents." (Goldstein, 1916, quoted by Weber, 1926)

"The school administrator of today [is] beset on every hand by book agents, wise and otherwise." (Doughton, 1917)

"Hundreds of new textbooks are published in the United States every year." (Herzberg, 1917)

"Much as our publishers of texts have been attacked on various grounds, few have questioned the fact that their enterprise and broadmindedness have contributed greatly to improving American education." ("Text-book Industry," 1918)

Continued on next page

Table 1.1 (Continued)

"For arousing newspaper furor, stimulating political clap-trap and breeding popular distrust, the adoption of textbooks has no equal in the whole range of school activities." (Shawkey, 1918)

"One purpose of the publishing business is to earn money, but if that were the only end the best publishers would not be in it." (Brown, 1919)

"It seems that when business and education conflict, business usually wins." (Coffman, 1919)

not be genuinely effective unless free textbooks were also available to all students.

Tash had personally been an advocate for free textbooks for over 30 years and identified cities such as Philadelphia and New York that had distributed free textbooks well before this era. He estimated that more than half of the textbooks being used in New England had been furnished free and that further expansion of free textbook policies was inevitable. Sympathetic to Tash's attitudes, Townsend (1891) observed that 10 to 20 percent of school age children had been deprived of an education because their parents could not afford the necessary textbooks. He approvingly quoted a New Hampshire superintendent who warned that universal education could never be achieved as long as textbooks had to be purchased by financially strapped parents.

In a list of states and cities that had implemented free textbook policies during the nineteenth century, Cox (1903) identified Massachusetts, Nebraska, Delaware, New Hampshire, Maine, New Jersey, Pennsylvania, Rhode Island, Vermont, Idaho, and Maryland. He also singled out several cities that had implemented free textbook policies in the early 1800s. Writing that same year, Waterman (1903) cited numerous cities, school districts, and states that were distributing free textbooks. Dexter (1904) observed that the majority of states were providing free textbooks for either all the children or at least those that were indigent. Two decades later, Hood (1922) reported that nearly all states provided books to indigent students, that many provided them to all secondary students, and that 39 states provided them to all elementary students.

Like many of the articles about free books that were written during this period, Waterman (1903) stressed the advantages of free materials. Although he also identified disadvantages, the negative arguments today do not seem persuasive. For example, he noted that some opponents of free books feared that diseases were being transmitted in the pages of used materials. At that time, this was a credible argument. As an example of the longevity of this concern, Figure 1.1 contains a 1929 advertisement for textbook covers that were being marketed to "promote sanitation."

Waterman developed nine convincing arguments to showcase the advantages of free books. His initial positive argument was that free textbooks lifted a great financial burden from parents. Like Waterman, McGregor (1908) also delineated the arguments surrounding free textbook policies. As was the case with Waterman's rhetoric, the logic opposing the free textbook policy today seems somewhat specious. For example, he noted that free textbook policies might destroy the concept of individual property. In contrast, his arguments in favor of free textbook policies were quite convincing. His initial argument stipulated that the mass purchasing of free textbooks reduced the prices of privately purchased books by 75 percent. The cost of textbooks in the late 1800s in Boston, $1.23 per student, was reduced to 70 cents just two years after adopting a free textbook policy (Marshall, 1895). This cost reduction enabled school administrators to supply textbooks to many students who otherwise would have been without them.

The need for textbook uniformity was another issue that was tied to free textbook programs. Writing little more than a decade into the twentieth century, Fitzpatrick (1912) had observed that extensive textbook publication transpired only because of the market created when schools required pupils to use identical books. Having made similar observations, Cornell (1888) had earlier reminisced that "some of us can remember when each child came to school supplied with such books as had come down to him through the careful hands of two or three generations, or had been given him by some kind-hearted neighbor" (p. 225). Cornell assured his readers that even in the late nineteenth century the benefits of common schoolbooks had been debated for more than a generation and that most teachers, administrators, and state legislators recognized them. By the early twentieth century, Dexter (1904) noted that every state except Alabama had adopted some procedure to assure uniform textbooks.

After reviewing the controversies about textbook uniformity, Dutton and Snedden (1909) concluded that the major issue was monetary. This was evident in those states that had adopted uniform textbook policies but not provided any assistance for purchasing textbooks. In a retrospective analysis of the arguments that had been made about free textbooks, Cook (1927) concluded that many supporters of free textbooks were not sincere and had encouraged this policy because they hoped it would eventually lead to uniform textbooks, for which it was more difficult to create a credible argument. After parenthetically acknowledging the many arguments in support of free textbooks, Cook observed wryly that the validity of these arguments was negatively correlated with their number. Among supporting arguments he noted convictions that free texts nurtured respect for public property, allowed mass purchasing at reduced prices, simplified adoption of new textbooks, assured that all students were ready at the beginning of a term, and increased the probability that books would be used systematically by the maximum number of learners. Arguments against free textbooks were that they were unhygienic, discouraged the development of private libraries, made excessive demands on public finances, increased the administrative responsibilities of the schools, and unfairly assisted students who received copies of books with the answers to problems already penciled in by previous users.

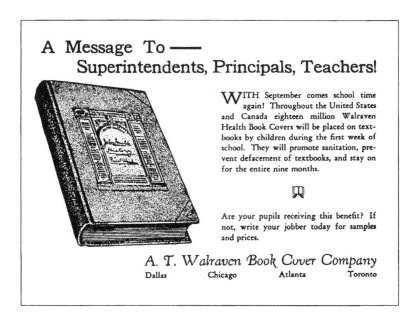

Figure 1.1 A 1929 Advertisement that Promoted a Connection Between Public Textbooks and Disease

State-Published Textbooks

As the educational publishing industry expanded during the late 1800s, teachers, parents, and legislators began to view textbooks as commercial products. It was inevitable that critics would investigate whether state governments could save money by producing these products themselves. While estimating costs for state-published materials, J. F. Brown (1915a) listed four factors that had contributed to the escalating prices of competitive textbooks: manufacturing costs, overhead charges, royalties, and publishers' profits. Writing a year later, Scott (1916) also acknowledged that state initiatives to publish textbooks were the direct response to increasing prices. As for his own reaction to these initiatives, he wrote that he refused to "enter the wilderness of figures" that the advocates of state textbook publishing had entered to rationalize their actions.

Educators opposed the state legislators who had begun to design procedures to curb excessive textbook payments. Cornell (1888) was an educational opponent who asked "shall the state, to throw off the incubus, itself enter the market, establish its own shops, gather its material, construct its various machines, fix the prices thereof, and enforce their use throughout its jurisdiction—establishing its depots of supplies, and its numerous agents of distribution, and its collectors and accountants?" (p. 232). Fearing that his readers might interpret this as a rhetorical question, Cornell responded "who can fail to answer—No!" Cornell was convinced that state publishers lacked the skills to develop and market textbooks. At an even more practical level, he speculated that, just in Pennsylvania, $2,500,000 had been invested in recent materials that would be sacrificed to make room for state-published books.

Cornell made his remarks at a meeting of the National Educational Association. Sprague (1888) followed him on the same program and characterized Cornell's ideas as "radically unsound." Sprague argued philosophically that because citizens were indistinguishable from their states, Cornell had erred by drawing an artificial dichotomy between the interest of the public and that of the states. Sprague suggested that appropriate measures, including the state publication of educational texts, were required to ensure that high textbook prices did not exclude children from schools. Sprague admonished Cornell that "by a refinement of cruelty, in some states attendance is made compulsory, but no provision made to spare the laceration of the feelings of the parent compelled to see his children reduced to paupers" (p. 235).

The most widely publicized incident of state publishing took place in California. At their annual meeting in 1883, the members of the California

State Teachers' Association resolved that state publication was "inexpedient and impracticable, and will if attempted result in great pecuniary loss to the state and expensive and unsatisfactory books to our schools" (quoted by Brown, 1915a, p. 41). Ignoring this advice, California did begin to publish its own textbooks. Bruce and Bruce (1925) recounted that almost every state did at some time consider state-published textbooks, but that only two states, California and Kansas, "were rash enough years ago to engage in such a hazardous project" (p. 67).

Faulkner (1900) described the passage of early legislation that authorized California to publish textbooks.

> The twenty-first session of the legislature of California met on December 6, 1875. On the third day of the session a bill entitled "An Act to prevent unnecessary changes in text-books in use in the public schools" was introduced in the senate. Its passage was expedited in both houses. Being promptly signed by the Governor it became a law just one week after its introduction in the senate. (p. 44)

Swett (1888) recounted that an 1884 amendment to the constitution authorized the state to adopt textbooks that would be edited by the State Board of Education, printed by the state printing office, and then sold to students at cost. However, Swett noted that by 1888 only several books had been published—three volumes from a set of readers, a spelling book, an arithmetic, a grammar, and a United States history. He indicated that not all of these books were being adopted and those that had been purchased were being used in only limited areas.

Chancellor (1913) provided a colorful account of the political events that accompanied the passing of an 1888 bill that went a step further and actually mandated state publication of all textbooks used in California's schools.

> It was in or about the year 1888 when the news of the bills to make all textbooks by state printing came by wire, by mail and by messengers to the eastern publishing houses of the time. They sent special agents by fast express trains to Sacramento and these agents reported that the bills were "strike bills" meant to force money out of the private publishers for pigeon-holing the bills in committee. Accordingly the special agents came back, leaving a vacuum, so they said, in which the bills would die of suffocation. But two bills passed and were signed by the governor. (p. 218)

Educators and politicians debated for decades about the efficiency of the California venture. In an 1888 report, the State Superintendent claimed that California-published textbooks were being produced for only one-third the price of privately published textbooks. The Superintendent crowed triumphantly that "hence no man will dare try to abort this great reform and saddle again on the people the grinding exaction under which they had heretofore groaned" (California State Superintendent, quoted by Jenks, 1906, p. 223). However, Faulkner (1900) chronicled the financial miscalculations and cost overruns made by California during the early years that it was publishing textbooks. He observed soberly that Californians had been unwise to approve this initiative because they had not reckoned on the taxes that were needed to support equipment and workers. Faulkner concluded that Californians had paid for their books twice, once at purchase and subsequently through taxation. In an editorial written nine years after Faulkner's account, Winship (1909) remarked that the California initiative had been undertaken solely to save money. Like Faulkner, he concluded that the twenty-year effort had failed because it had not resulted in any genuine savings. Winship also quoted an extensive testimonial from the secretary of the California Textbook Commission, who charged that the state-published books were not only expensive but inferior to commercial textbooks.

Chancellor (1913) wrote that persons in many states were stirred by the textbook initiative in California and supported or opposed the extension of that model to their states. The original plans in California had directed children's parents to purchase books published by the state. In 1913, new legislation was passed that required California's schools to buy state-published textbooks and then distribute these free to all students in the public schools ("School text-books," 1915). A year later, Evans (1914) warned the citizens of Georgia against approving any plan similar to that in California, where citizens had become mired in a system from which most wished to escape.

Evans advised his readers to avoid not only the California model but that of Kansas. Although the Kansas publication of textbooks was approved in 1913, McCray (1914) recorded background details about a bill similar to California's that had almost been passed during the nineteenth century.

> The lobbyists who besieged the Kansas legislature of 1897, urging the enactment of the state uniformity law, it later developed, were interested in selling their wares. A local job printing house had secured the right to publish a series of readers and other texts written by Kansas authors. This was an incentive for a get-together movement by publisher and author. The proposition was alluring in that it offered a market for home authorship. The argument was put forth that Kansas possessed educators capable of writing all the texts needed in the schools of the state, and that these should be printed in Kansas. (p. 200)

The inclusion of the preceding account, as well as the title of his article, "Kansas, Wise and Otherwise," alerted readers to McCray's skepticism about the value of state publication. McCray recounted that the 1913 Kansas legislature was predisposed toward state publication of textbooks, and this commitment prevailed despite the advice of the educational community. Chancellor (1913) summarized other state and city initiatives that were pending after Kansas resolved to publish its own textbooks.

> With California publishing state school books and Kansas just entering upon such publication, with Chicago making a speller of which the first edition is to be 175,000 copies, with New Orleans moving fast in the same direction, with the national government and many states and cities already publishing syllabuses of courses, pamphlets of methods, volumes on entertainments, holidays, agriculture, school-houses and birds, and with bills in a dozen state legislatures to establish state printing plants and resolutions in as many city boards and country commissions, the question as to what attitude every educator should take is immediate and practical. (p. 161)

Chancellor answered the question posed in the preceding passage by advising those states and cities that were proposing to publish their own materials to pause and reconsider.

A year after Chancellor had published this report, an editorial in the *Nation* ("Textbooks and the State," 1915) concluded that the movement for state publication of textbooks had never gained any great national headway. Georgia was among the many states that had already rejected initiatives for state publication and the editorialist was wary only of Alabama, which was undecided. The following year, Brown (1915b) characterized the prevailing attitude when he wrote of state-published textbooks that "the choice seems to lie between inferior books at prices that show no saving when all the cost factors are included and the best books at prices that permit a fair publishers' profit" (p. 485).

However, some did not agree. For example, McNeal (1915) disputed Brown's argument, pointing out that state publishing in Kansas had saved $200,000 annually, resulted in books of superior quality, and prevented publishing firms' lobbyists from corrupting legislators and teachers. Five years later, Hall-Quest (1920) challenged McNeal's argument. He argued that because most students resold their textbooks after they had used them, any estimate of the cost for commercial textbooks needed to be reduced by the amount of money that was predictably returned to students during this reselling. Including this adjustment in the financial equation, he reasoned that Kansas-produced textbooks were significantly more expensive than commercial materials.

Reports questioning the state publication of textbooks continued to appear from 1916 through 1920. Wright (1916) wrote that the state of Washington had the best elementary schools and that this was partially due to

Figure 1.2 Political Cartoon Linking State-Published Textbooks to
Misinformed News Reports

its insistence on the use of commercial materials. An editorial about the state
publication of textbooks in Kansas ("Criticism of Kansas," 1917) expressed
the author's frustration at that state's repeated refusals to provide the financial
data needed to accurately document expenses and savings. Two years later,
Shirer (1919) bitterly complained that state publication in Kansas would
continue irrespective of its cost effectiveness because "the forces behind it will
try to keep the mill grinding, whatever the grist" (p. 467). An article by Avery
(1919) expressed the same concern about the failure of California's printing
office to furnish complete evidence. A political cartoon that accompanied a

report (Bruce & Bruce, 1925) from this period linked state-published textbooks to misinformed reporting about the actual costs of privately published textbooks (Figure 1.2).

At one time it seemed that many states would publish their own textbooks. Webster (1897) recorded that bills to authorize state publication had been introduced in 10 states just during the late 1890s. Despite early predictions, only California and Kansas actually did so. Cook (1927) concluded that the majority of persons eventually recognized that California and Kansas had produced materials that were vastly inferior but only somewhat cheaper. Three years later, Davis (1930) questioned whether state-published textbooks had resulted in any true savings after one considered that state reports had consistently failed to acknowledge actual expenses for equipment, labor, buildings, and maintenance.

Writing two decades after Davis, Burnett (1952) indicated that California and Kansas were still publishing their own textbooks. He reported that four other states—Florida, Georgia, Indiana, and Louisiana—had legislation authorizing them to do so. Indiana had attempted to publish its own textbooks but then given up after only a few years. Florida had decided to substitute a hybrid plan that promoted local authorship through cooperative agreements with private publishers. Georgia and Louisiana had never acted upon their schemes. Noting that the state publication had been implemented to save money, Burnett continued to question whether any savings had resulted. He also faulted California for failing to supply the complete sets of textbooks promised for the schools. He thought that the problems created by this failure were so severe that no amount of savings, even had there been any, would have justified it. Unable to rationalize the California plan, he discouraged other states from following it.

Growth of the Textbook Market

Publishers increased textbook production because they were guaranteed a steady, high income from the many districts that had implemented uniform or free textbook policies. Barnard (1863a, 1863b, 1863c, 1864a, 1864b, 1865) produced a series of inventories of American textbooks from the middle 1800s. Though his extensive inventories of the textbooks that had been written, published, or used in the United States were incomplete, they still identified hundreds of textbooks in each installment. Presenting a different type of data to illustrate the growth of textbook publishing, Richey (1931) summarized the number of elementary and secondary school textbooks that had been written by decades. For example, during the decade beginning in 1876, 200 textbooks were published. During the next decade, 260 books were printed. However, during the two-decade span from 1896 to 1916, over 800 textbooks were printed.

Increasing Prices of Textbooks

Market growth and increasing prices ensured financial success for commercial textbook publishers. However, critics argued that publishers' increasing income was also the result of devious practices through which they misrepresented their true production expenses and then overcharged customers. Records from the late nineteenth century revealed trends in pricing that alarmed critics and then made them suspicious. For example, Townsend (1891) listed the projected costs for the state-produced textbooks that California authorized in 1883 and contrasted these with the actual costs of those books. He indicated that a speller, originally estimated to cost 8 cents, had required 25 cents to produce. First-, second-, and third-level readers, respectively, estimated to cost 9, 17, and 24 cents, had cost 25, 15, and 33 cents. The most dramatic discrepancy had been in history books, which though projected to cost 20 cents, had required 70 cents. Also citing data from the reports that had been made at the time California's legislators decided to publish their own textbooks, Faulkner (1900) indicated the average costs of the textbooks that could be purchased from publishers during the early 1880s. As examples, the spellers were priced at 18 cents, beginning readers at 20 cents, intermediate readers at 50 cents, advanced readers at 85 cents, arithmetic books at one dollar, grammars at one dollar and 25 cents, and history textbooks at one dollar and 25 cents.

McGregor (1908) estimated that the per pupil expense for all textbooks under a free textbook system was just 50 cents. Since this was a mathematical average, he pointed to some cities where books were even cheaper, such as La Cross, Wisconsin, at 23 cents per pupil. The cities on which he had collected data exhibited a wide range of costs, as indicated by a district in Rhode Island that was spending 66 cents per pupil. The superintendent of the Jersey City schools (Marshall, 1895) estimated that the per pupil cost for books and stationery averaged between 50 cents and $1.25 throughout a long period during which the district had funded free textbooks.

Hilton (1913) listed the Ohio prices for books used during the initial eight grades of school.

Primer .... $ .20
First reader .... .24
Second reader .... .30
Third reader .... .41
Fourth reader .... .50
Fifth reader .... .58
Elementary geography .... .50
Advanced geography 1.03
United States history .... .83
Elementary grammar .... .33
Advanced grammar .... .50
Copy books .... .25
Possibly one elementary history at .... .50
(p. 369)

George Brown (1915) reported that in the large cities that furnished free textbooks, no city averaged more than $1.60 annually per child, while some cities spent as little as 60 cents. Brown added editorially that "for every child in school there is also being spent $300 a year for booze, $150 a year for cigars, $50 a year for moving pictures, and $20 a year for candy" and concluded that, by comparison, "school books do not cost so much as we are sometimes led to suppose" (p. 566).

An early twentieth-century report about the prices of textbooks ("Quality and Cost," 1915) noted that though profits from textbooks had increased as a result of expanded adoptions, the cost of individual textbooks had actually decreased since 1885.

> Notwithstanding the advance in the quality of text-books, their cost has decreased. There has been an average reduction of more than ten percent. in the past twenty-five years, and some books have been reduced in price much more than this. The reduction has come about steadily and surely. There has been no fluctuation; the downward trend has proceeded steadily through boom times—when many manufacturers have benefitted by increased prices—and through hard times, and even the constantly increasing cost of labor and materials has not arrested this progress. The chief economic explanation of all this is undoubtedly the competition of the many independent text-book publishers and the invention of labor-saving devices in printing and binding. (p. 681)

That same report justified the prices of textbooks through a graph that compared the total amount spent nationally on textbooks with expenditures on other products such as tobacco, soda, and candy. The graph revealed that more than $400,000,000 was being sent annually on tobacco products, while schoolbook expenditures did not exceed $12,000,000. The report also contained a table comparing the differential expenses for producing the printing plates for novels, elementary school history books, and high-school history textbooks. Although a high school history textbook would retail for $1.50 a copy, the initial cost of development was $10,000. In contrast, a popular novel, which also sold for $1.50 a copy, required only $1,275 for setup.

Some proponents of textbooks admitted that the increasing profits were to some extent the result of higher prices. Winship (1915) acknowledged and defended escalating prices when he insisted that "if the school books cost as much as teachers' salaries, we should still have them" (p. 285). To muster support, he reminded educators that "no scheme or device or plan of teaching anything has ever spread it so efficiently very far until it was put into a text-book" and that "it would cost a thousand times as much, yea, ten thousand times as much, to promote the general adoption of any great improvement in teaching by the visitation scheme as by the text-book plan" (pp. 285–286). He concluded acerbically that those who purchased cheap textbooks were the types of persons who would buy discounted, rancid eggs or shop for tattered clothing at rummage sales.

Increased Profits from Textbooks

Although information about the prices of textbooks had been available, it was not until the very end of the nineteenth century that publishers began to summarize their sales from textbooks. After reviewing these data, Madison (1966) noted that total annual sales from textbooks had increased from $7,400,000 in 1897 to $17,275,000 by 1913. These estimates were commensurate with those of Hall-Quest (1920), who examined data in the 1910 Census Bureau Bulletin and a 1911–1912 report form the U.S. Commission of Education to estimate that year's public school textbook expenditures at $12,000,000. Writing during this period, Ginn (1910) figured that the total textbook trade in the United States was between $9,000,000 and $12,000,000 annually. Another report from the early twentieth century ("Facts about School," 1913) calculated that the total annual textbook sales in the United States was $15,000,000. Although he looked only at the textbook market in Virginia, Monahan (1915) reported dramatic growth from 1911 to 1915, when sales increased from $147,000 to $215,700.

A report during World War I ("Text-book Industry," 1918) estimated that total sales of textbooks, even when one included the burgeoning market for college textbooks, had not yet reached $20,000,000. The author of an earlier World War I editorial ("Textbooks and the State," 1915) calculated that 2 percent of the total educational budget, approximately $17,000,000, had been spent that year on public school textbooks. The same editorialist also provided a testimonial about the fierce rivalry among publishers. However, unlike those pro-textbook critics who thought that competition contributed to low textbook prices, this editorialist wrote that the competition among publishers "was so keen, their methods in some cases were so shady, that not only politicians, but well meaning folk, were tempted to ask themselves whether there must not be huge profits in a business that could support such extravagant methods of unloading its product" ("Textbooks and the State," 1915, p. 322).

Davis (1930) consulted financial reports from the California State Department of Education for the 1927–1928 academic year and determined that the cost of state-published textbooks exceeded $430,000. Even this figure did not include the payments for the many supplementary textbooks on which the California schools relied. Davis also revealed numerous indirect costs that should have been included in the summary estimates that were compiled by California and that would have substantially inflated those estimates.

Effect of World War I

During World War I, textbook publishing was influenced by financial constraints. In an effort to restrict the production of nonessential materials, the War Industries Board mandated a 50 percent reduction in textbook publishing ("Text-Book Industry," 1918). This harsh United States policy was in contrast to that of Great Britain, where textbooks had been exempted from the restrictions that were imposed on other types of books. However, some critics expressed confidence in the American plan. One editorialist ("Economizing in Text-books," 1918) wrote that the actions of the War Industries Board were appropriate and he hoped that the pressure would continue after the war to ensure "somewhat less extravagant" textbook budgets.

Also writing about the wartime regulatory movement, Henry Dewey (1920) observed that publishers were not initially upset by the production restrictions because they were implemented in a careful, incremental manner. However, from 1915 to 1920, and particularly during 1919 through 1920, the situation changed. Dewey elaborated about some of the disconcerting changes that he detected in textbook pricing regulations:

From one end of the country to the other we read of the "vicious circle" of increasing cost of production and the high cost of living. Each is claimed to be the cause of the other. Probably both are cause and effect. The ordinary manufacturer, unhampered by the state laws or listing, simply raises his prices when cost of production increases. His lot is easy enough. His price at all times bears a fixed ratio to cost of production. The schoolbook publisher cannot adjust his prices in this easy going way. Along in 1914 or 1916, perhaps he listed his books in a state for a fixed period. He did not sell them but simply quoted a price at which he would furnish them to a school district in that state if the district would adopt a book and agree to use it for a period of years. Under the provisions of the listing laws of these states, while they differ in many other particulars, there is one uniform requirement, to-wit: a book must be sold at the "lowest price" at which it is sold anywhere in the United States. (p. 31)

Because price regulations prevented textbooks from being retailed at their true cost, Dewey protested that schools were unable to buy the best books. Convinced that the interests of publishers and schools were identical, he argued that states should eliminate any remnants of wartime textbook pricing.

Ohler (1924) was another critic who observed that the growth of textbook publishing had been restricted by wartime manufacturing costs. Writing just two years after Dewey, he was sure that these restrictions had already been effectively eliminated. He advised textbook publishers who were not earning sufficient profits to refrain from blaming government regulations and instead to adopt proven sales strategies. World War I era advertisements from major publishers were intended to entice progressive educators. For example, an advertisement for an English book from Ginn and Company (Figure 1.3) emphasized key elements of the progressive approach to writing instruction, such as appeal to student interest, fresh learning activities, socialization, an emphasis on oral language, and the incorporation of play. Another advertisement, this one from the Century Company about one of its civics textbooks, was linked to a statement by Woodrow Wilson, a politician who shared attitudes about world peace and international cooperation that were similar to those of many progressive educators.

Textbook advertisements for food, soap, perfume, and stock feeds were additional marketing strategies that some publishers used during this period. However, Ohler (1924) urged companies to maintain their professional decorum and avoid the temptation to bolster profits with faddish advertisements.

Figure 1.3 A 1917 Advertisement for English Language Textbooks

World War II and the Postwar Period

Reid (1969) was an editor for a major publisher during the 1930s. He reported that the Depression had affected the trade division of his firm much harder than the textbook division. In fact, textbook sales had been surging ahead so strongly that only during 1932, the gloomiest point in the Depression, did his company fail to show financial growth. This profitable pattern continued for Reid's firm and most other companies until the beginning of World War II.

Though the production of textbooks may have never been genuinely threatened, their profitability was somewhat restricted during World War II, when production costs increased by 100 percent. However, Lehmann-Haupt, Wroth, and Silver (1951) observed that the high costs and prices did subside and that by 1950 prices had receded to a point that was only 20 to 35 percent above the prewar levels. They quoted the director of a university press who warned that under such circumstances publishers were trying to ensure success by releasing only essential materials, such as reference books and textbooks. From a complementary viewpoint, McKeon, Merton, and Gelhorn (1957) observed that publishers were attempting to assure that their materials would be adopted by providing textbook selection boards with products that were custom-tailored to the demands set by those boards.

Textbooks continued to demonstrate remarkable market growth after World War II. Mayer (1962) noted that in 1960 approximately 50 publishers had been responsible for 230 million dollars in textbook sales. He calculated this as an increase of 100 million dollars over sales in 1954. However, he judged that this additional revenue was the result of a greater number of students in schools rather than increased expenditures on textbooks per student. Because of the opportunities signaled by the greater number of students in schools, Wall Street brokers had begun to regard textbook publishing as a growth industry and the prices of textbook stocks soared out of proportion to their earnings.

Other reports documented the growth of the textbook business after World War II and during the second half of the twentieth century. Madison (1966) noted that, though the total sales from textbooks had been $17,275,000 in 1913, this amount had burgeoned to $131,000,000 by 1947. Without placing a value on sales, an international committee (UNESCO, 1959) estimated that 44,000,000 textbooks had been purchased that year in the United States alone. By the middle of the 1960s, Brammer (1967) calculated that the annual sale of textbooks and educational materials had climbed to $508,850,000.

Although the precise growth of the textbook trade was difficult to chart because of the different types of data reported in financial documents, a 1976 issue of *Publishers Weekly* provided multiple perspectives on the expansion. For example, one of the authors, Dessauer (1976), revealed the overall health of the publishing industry when he noted that it had increased 25 times in dollar volume during the preceding four decades. In that same issue, Nordberg (1976) computed that elementary and high-school textbooks had captured 39 percent of the 1974 book market and 38 percent of the 1975 market. Dessauer observed that the sales of elementary and secondary textbooks had increased by more than 29 percent from 1971 to 1975, with total revenues exceeding $600,000,000 in 1975.

After examining demographic data, Noble (1976) cautioned that the number of children entering the schools was about to decline. However, he observed optimistically that this decline would be offset by a trend toward increasing per capita textbook expenditures. This prediction was accurate, and the amount of money being spent on textbooks had expanded by 1980. Marquand (1985b) wrote that more than a billion dollars was being spent annually on textbooks and that educational publishing was so profitable that more than 60 firms exclusively produced textbooks. Because five large companies accounted for 40 percent of the books being produced, Marquand did question the long-term prospects for textbook publishing competition. This cautious observation by Marquand had been made years earlier when Bowler (1978) reported that seven of the 150 companies competing in the elementary-secondary textbook market were earning 57 percent of all revenues. Moreover, three years before Bowler's observation, Barber (1975) had noted that the top ten textbook publishers were responsible for half of all sales.

Houghton Mifflin was one of the large educational publishers. Fox (1985) interviewed the chairman of that corporation who indicated that 80 percent of his company's total sales came from textbooks. Fox also noted that the profit margin for textbooks was a lucrative 14 percent. As a comparative frame of reference, the profit margins for the automobile industry and the retail industry during this period were respectively 5.5 percent and 3.2 percent. Table 1.2 (p. 22) contains mid-twentieth-century quotations about textbooks as products. Many of these quotes refer to the expansion of the textbook publishing industry during this period.

Table 1.2　　Mid-Twentieth-Century Criticism of Textbooks as Products

"Vast numbers of textbooks are being published each year." (Dill, 1921)

"The school book question has been and is the most mischievous unsettled educational question before the people today." (McCullough, 1922)

"Too often a salesman's speech, the number of cents each book costs, or a good dinner followed by a pleasing theater party are given too much weight in the selection of school textbooks." (Fowlkes, 1923)

"It is universally recognized that America produces the best textbooks in the world." (Donovan, 1924)

"We are fed up on [criticism about] 'bookgraft,' 'state adoption scandals,' [and] 'corruption of school officials.'" (Douglas, 1924)

"Experience has taught…that a competitive school book business, such as we have in this country, makes for efficient authorship and reasonable prices." (Bruce & Bruce, 1925)

"Of the making of textbooks there has been no end." (Green, 1926)

"Considerable education is gained from schools, from books, and from fellow teachers, and also not a little from the publishing company representatives." (Reese, 1928)

"New textbooks are numerous and expensive." (Leighton, 1928)

"Good textbooks are plentiful and cheap." (Tidwell, 1928)

"Superior textbooks are almost certain to cost more than inferior ones." (Whipple, 1929)

"A number of instances of bribery or coercion by book companies have recently occurred….[but] in justice to the publishers it should be said that school men themselves are often not unreceptive to 'favor' from publishers." (Beale, 1936)

"A textbook salesman remarked to the writer one day that in a certain large city in the East the man who had the best liquor sold the most books!" (Stillwell, 1950)

"The textbook business, as businesses go, is a small one." (Saveth, 1952)

"The supplying of textbooks to the thirty-seven million children and adults in our school systems makes the textbook industry a major business." (Blanshard, 1955)

Escalating Costs of Textbook Production

Despite high profits, the development costs for textbooks were also high. These costs were incurred as publishers were forced to hire larger and more specialized staffs to design and market superior school materials. The revised edition of McGuffey's *Eclectic Reader* (McGuffey, 1920) was an example of materials that had raised aesthetic and pedagogical standards. Figure 1.4 (p. 24) illustrates the impressive workmanship that was the hallmark of these readers.

The costs of producing and marketing superior school materials prevented many companies from competing in the textbook market. In the early part of the century, Middleton (1911) was able to document 80 textbook publishers. However, he observed that one of these firms had a list of almost 3,000 selections and that four other dominating publishers had comparably exhaustive inventories. Additionally, Middleton observed that several states were "practically owned" by select publishers. Despite many notorious business abuses by textbook publishers, he still concluded that competition in this industry was visible and viable.

The increasingly extensive personnel required to produce textbooks certainly did limit competition. Brown (1919) described the large and specialized staffs that successful post–World War I publishers needed to maintain.

> The publisher is not dependent upon his own experiences and observation alone for his information. Through his editorial department and his field agents he is in constant touch with the best that is being thought and done in the educational field. These assistants consist for the most part of capable men and women who have had successful experiences as teachers and school administrators. They are intimately acquainted with the work of the school and with the leaders in their respective territories. They know the men who are writing books or who ought to be doing it. So well informed are they that many teachers and administrators welcome their visits because of the information they bring concerning means, methods, and successful accomplishments in the educational field. While they are selling books and counseling with teachers they are gathering and sifting information which is of material assistance to the publisher in planning for new books and making needed revisions of old ones. (Brown, 1919, pp. 384–385)

Other twentieth-century reporters echoed Brown's observations about the need for the expanded and specialized textbook staffs. Davis (1930) reported that the development of a widely used arithmetic series had cost more than $25,000. He noted that a publisher of a popular language arts series had spent $15,000 just for typesetting, illustrations, and electroplates. That publisher also

LESSON XIII.

Tŏm   tŏp   Kĭt′tў′ş

ăt

băck

lŏŏk

g͞ŏŏd   dŏll   thĭnk   spŏt

th   n   ŏŏ

Look at Tom and his dog.
The dog has a black spot on
his back. Do you think he is
a good dog?

Tom has a big top, too. It
is on the box with Kitty's doll.

Figure 1.4 The McGuffey Readers Set High Standards for Textbook Publishing

paid $60,000 a year to maintain a large editorial staff that devoted one-sixth of its time to school textbooks. Writing 30 years after these reporters, Jennings (1964) noted that each of the large textbook houses maintained a staff that "could provide a complete faculty for a fine education department in a good college." He added that diverse well-educated employees were essential for developing the most profitable books, which were those that would be adopted more than once and that would dominate for a generation.

The coauthor of a history textbook developed during the 1950s (Bragdon, 1969) reported that the publisher's initial investment in plates, maps, illustrations, charts, and other production requirements had at that time increased to more than $250,000. Black (1967) reported about a science series on which the publisher had spent $525,000 prior to publication. Less than a decade later, Broudy (1975) estimated that the development of a typical English textbook required $50,000 to $100,000, that a social studies book with maps and art would require five times as much, and that a reading series would cost $1,000,000. A decade later, Fox (1985) alluded to a 1980s basal reading program that had cost more than $15,000,000 and recounted how one large textbook publisher had nearly gone bankrupt after the failure of its basal reading series.

Author royalties also contributed to textbook expenses. Davis (1985) described a social studies textbook for which Houghton Mifflin had paid the author $50,000 as an advance against royalties. The firm anticipated that this author would receive another $130,000 on the sales of 100,000 copies during the initial year of sales. Fox (1985) calculated that author royalties had risen to 5.3 percent of the total cost for textbooks. He compared this expense with the other costs such as printing, binding, and paper—22.7 percent, editorial services—6.2 percent, production and plant operations—7.7 percent, delivery—7.3 percent, and administrative operations—7.6 percent.

As a hedge against the increasing costs of production, publishing houses began to merge into larger businesses with greater financial security. In his history of textbook publishing, Brammer (1967) indicated that textbook publishers had been struck with merger fever during three periods. These large-scale mergers transpired at the end of the nineteenth century, at the beginning of the twentieth century, and during the 1960s.

> After half a century of relative stability, the fever returned. Publishers from various areas of publishing have combined to effect overhead economies and to balance income fluctuations. Newspaper, periodical, movie, and electronic concerns have set up combinations with textbook and trade publishers to broaden their scope within the overall field of communication. Industries outside the communications field with excess profits to invest have been looking long and hard at the relatively stable

textbook publishing income. Financial writers are fond of projecting textbook publishing potentials mathematically upward in relation to the population explosion. Textbook publishers stocks are now listed and traded actively on the stock exchange. (p. 348)

As an indication of frenzied reorganizing, Redding (1963) listed 26 major publishing mergers that took place just between 1958 and 1962.

A fourth period of mergers was evident in the 1980s. These consolidations were engineered to ensure that even the larger publishers had the resources to prosper in the highly expensive venture into which textbook publication had evolved ("Book Publishing," 1987). Rothman (1989) reported about the merger of three firms to produce the largest textbook publisher in the United States, the Macmillan/McGraw-Hill School Publishing Company. Despite the financial prudence of such consolidations, Rothman indicated that some educators were worried that the mergers would reduce innovation in educational materials. However, such anxieties seemed negligible after the cost for developing a single basal reading series in the late 1980s had risen to $40,000,000 (Sewall & Cannon, 1991). In view of such expense, it was hardly surprising when even established textbook publishers indicated that they felt compelled to merge.

Although the increasing prices of textbooks limited the ability of some publishers to compete in this expensive market, higher prices also ensured that the profits that accrued to successful firms would be substantial. Table 1.3 contains late twentieth-century quotations that referred to textbooks as products. Many of these quotes highlight the increasing expenses and profits associated with textbook publishing during this era.

Summary

The profitability of textbook publishing rose throughout the nineteenth century. These profits were connected to the size of the market, which increased dramatically after reformers began to argue that public education could achieve its full potential only if students were assured free textbooks. Advocates of free textbooks pointed to the injustice that children endured in educational systems where even poor families were responsible for purchasing educational materials. They also highlighted the advantages of buying books for the lowest possible prices, which was possible only when textbooks were purchased in large quantities by school districts.

The potential conflict of interest created by profits convinced some critics that publishers had abandoned the pedagogical objectives for learning

Table 1.3   Late Twentieth-Century Criticism of Textbooks as Products

"Textbook publishers, whose industry has an estimated annual sales total of $300 million, have a business investment to protect." (Hechinger, 1960)

"Profits are greater in this field [of textbook publishing], and risks smaller." (Mayer, 1962)

"Since publishers are businessmen, who must act out the myth that the customer is always right—even when the customer is obviously dead wrong—we would be foolish to expect reform from that quarter." (Margolis, 1965)

"The textbook publisher in America is forced to be a vigorous, if not rugged, example of independent enterprise." (Brammer, 1967)

"The textbook industry is, by any measure, a midget." (Williamson, 1979)

"It costs millions of dollars to produce a new basal reading series." (English, 1980)

"About 65 companies fight for a piece of the $1.4 billion that elementary and secondary schools will spend this year on textbooks." (Davis, 1985)

"The development of a basal reading program can take up to five years, and depending upon the size of the company and the scope of the program can cost $10–15 million." (Osborn & Stein, 1985)

"Tried and true textbooks throw off heaps of cash." ("Book Publishing," 1987)

"Textbook publishers are not in business for their own amusement or to satisfy some abstract notion of the public good—profits count." (Sewall, 1987)

"In the United States, the publishing of textbooks is a billion-dollar enterprise." (Chall & Conard, 1991)

"[The Texas Board of Education] is looking at $1.8 billion in projected costs for textbooks over the next six years." ("Texas May Drop," 1997)

"Secondary school texts average $40 each, with some of them going to $100 a piece." ("The Textbook Audit," 2000)

---

materials. Educators with a strong capitalistic philosophy retorted that a free market actually guaranteed that the best learning materials were available. Not persuaded by this retort, legislators became proponents of state-published textbooks. The most famous and controversial effort by a state to publish its own textbooks transpired in California. Although defenders of the California initiative alleged that it saved money, opponents judged that the books were inferior to commercial materials. Additionally, opponents noted that the California books, when one factored in the costs of equipment and personnel, were actually more expensive than the commercial materials.

Throughout the twentieth century, the prices of textbooks increased noticeably. Publishers rationalized the prices by pointing to the massive amount of capital that they had invested in writing, producing, field-testing, and marketing. However, in the final analysis, textbook publishing prospered in spite of increased prices because it was able to continually produce a product that both teachers and the public valued.

CHAPTER TWO

Textbooks as Propaganda—
The Nationalistic Era

Legislative censoring of textbooks was especially noticeable during wars and periods of threatened conflict. Conservative critics supported these measures because they were worried that school materials were eroding patriotic values. Although liberal critics endorsed censorship as well, they advocated restrictions on jingoistic books that could predispose students toward war.

Early Efforts to Legislate Nationalism in Textbooks

Though early twentieth-century nationalism became a lightning rod for textbook critics, neither the nationalism nor the censorship it attracted was unprecedented. Knight (1949) drew a parallel between the nineteenth-century opposition to textbooks and the resistance to European education demonstrated by eighteenth-century southern colonists. During the nineteenth century, southerners transferred this opposition from European educators to northern textbook publishers. Knight quoted a resolution from the Educational Association of the Confederate States renouncing dependence on books that were authored by persons who "now seek our subjugation." He then documented laws in the post–Civil War South prohibiting textbooks that depicted southern states in an unflattering manner. Also reviewing the nineteenth-century legislative movement to regulate the textbooks used in the South, Pierce (1929) had observed that this movement persisted until the beginning of World War I when it was dissipated by a national trend toward unification.

Lehmann-Haupt, Wroth, and Silver (1951) used eighteenth-century incidents to establish a perspective on twentieth-century events. They noted that John Peter Senger's 1734 acquittal on charges that he had abused his newspaper became an early validation for freedom of the press. After citing this colonial incident, they concluded that the press in the United States was then comparatively unmolested. They qualified their remark about undisturbed freedom with the adverb "comparatively" because they were able to identify several later examples of legislative pressures upon textbook publishers. In one of these incidents, the 1948 California State Senate attempted to suppress a controversial series of social studies textbooks.

Knight (1952) described attempts to regulate textbooks through legislative efforts that had originated during the 1800s, continued into the twentieth century, and approached a peak after World War I. Writing soon after World War I, Douglas (1924) agreed that the war had created regulatory pressures. A bill introduced into the 1923 New York legislature illustrated these pressures.

> No textbook shall be used or designated for use in the schools of any city, union, free school district or common school district of the state which
> (a) ignores, omits, discounts, or in any manner belittles, ridicules, falsifies, distorts, questions, doubts, or denies the events leading up to the Declaration of American Independence, or connected with the American Revolution, or the Spirit and determination with which the United States of America has established, defended, and maintained its rights as a free nation against foreign interference, encroachment, and aggression, or
> (b) ignores, omits discounts, or an any manner belittles, ridicules, falsifies, distorts, questions, doubts, or denies the deeds and accomplishments of the noted American patriots, or questions the worthiness of their motives, or casts aspersions on their lives. ("New York Bill on History," 1923, p. 349).

The bill from which the preceding passage was extracted enjoined the New York Commissioner of Education to withhold funds from guilty schools. Six years after the drafting of this legislation, a tariff bill was introduced into the U.S. Senate to regulate the national book trade. The bill was designed to prohibit "any book, pamphlet, paper, writing advertisement, circular, print, picture or drawing containing any matter advocating or urging treason, insurrection or forcible resistance to any law of the United States, or containing any threat to take the life of, or inflict bodily harm upon the President of the United States or any person" (quoted in "Tariff Bill's Prohibition," 1929, p. 407).

Not distressed by the legislative restrictions on textbooks, Douglas (1924) judged that the regulations had largely been incorporated into everyday life in ways that the public needed and even wanted. Other critics, however, did not disguise their disgruntlement. An editorial that had appeared originally in *New York World* decried the excessive regulation that had been precipitated by wartime and postwar paranoia. The editorial warned of the dangers posed by "non-combatants who went mad during the war" and who had tried to "censor languages here, history there, science somewhere else" ("Decision for Liberty," 1923, p. 669). Excessive regulation was the motivation for forming the Save-Our-Schools Committee, which pledged to ensure that schools did not become "subjects for propaganda by special interests, groups or causes"

(Wellington, 1929). Jane Addams and John Dewey were among the 70 influential activists who founded this committee.

Nationalism in Textbooks after World War I

Even before the war, expressions of nationalism in textbooks had helped allay postwar fears about international danger. The following passage from an early social studies book (Semple, 1903) was neither remarkable for its rococo rhetoric nor its unqualified nationalism.

> The Atlantic has given us near access to Europe and the "American invasion" has followed. The Pacific has opened to us, though at longer range, the markets of the Orient, and the flag has been set up on an outlying fragment of the Asiatic continent. "Enthroned between her subject seas," the United States has by reason of her large area and her geographical location the most perfect conditions for attaining preeminence in the commerce of the world ocean. (p. 435)

Although most readily discernible in history and government textbooks, nationalistic bias was exhibited in other materials as well. The following passage is from an early reading textbook (Carroll & Brooks, 1906):

> Girls, will you play soldier?
> Mary, here is a flag.
> Carry the flag in front.
> You lead the soldiers.
> Helen, carry the drum.
> Carry my gun, John.
> March behind Helen.
> I will march behind you.
> Beat the drum, Helen. (p. 32)

The nationalistic theme of this text was obvious. Supplementary textbooks, such as one by Serl and Pelo (1919), contained patriotic passages and illustrations to complement social studies textbooks.

Conducting a study of textbook nationalism for his master's thesis at Yale, Lew (1923) stipulated that he was trying to ascertain the degree to which the attitudes of American children toward China might be influenced by their educational materials. He wrote in a restrained style that the students' attitudes themselves were "far from encouraging" and gave the following example:

> A Yale man was once confronted at the entrance of the Dining Hall by a school boy who was returning from his school for lunch, passing through the Campus. "Are you a Jap?" "No," said the Yale man. "Then you are a Chinaman, eh? Are you just as bad or worse than a Jap?" "What do you mean?" The child answered, "You Chinamen eat snakes, dogs, and do lots of horrible things, don't you?" "Where did you learn that?" "At school," was the swift reply. (p. 10)

After citing anecdotal evidence as well numerous examples of nationalistic bias in textbooks, Lew concluded that "some improvements are urgently needed" (p. 149).

Lew's analysis of nationalistic bias in school materials was similar to other studies completed after World War I. Instead of concentrating on China, Schuyler (1918) lamented the unfair treatment of Britain in U.S. textbooks. He pointedly cited Thomas Paine, the Revolutionary era patriot, who had remarked that American "children in the streets are from their cradle bred to consider [Britain] as their only foe" (Paine, quoted by Schuyler, 1918, p. 189). Schuyler asked passionately when "popular education in general, and the teaching of history in particular, foster true or false patriotism; shall it promote international cooperation, justice, and peace, or self-entolling nationalism, rivalry, and war?" (p. 190). From a similar perspective, Eagleton (1918) also warned that one-sided textbook reporting was suppressing opportunities for a fraternal relationship with Great Britain. Many popular American history textbooks (e.g., Fite, 1919) contained a picture by Paul Revere that depicted the Boston Massacre. Interesting because of its patriot artist as well as its subject, this illustration appeared in virtually every textbook from this era. Needless to say, this type of one-sided imagery was precisely the type that Anglophiles wished to discourage.

Blanshard (1955) pointed out that critics who were attacking as well as those who were defending anti-British educational materials were passionate and political. For just as some individuals were worried that anti-British materials were undermining prospects for international cooperation, a group of American nationalists was just as fearful that pro-British textbooks would erode the patriotic sentiments of American youths. Even textbooks that highlighted incidents in which the two nations had cooperated were likely to be misunderstood as dangerously pro-British. The following reconciliatory passage is taken from an American history textbook (Muzzey, 1911):

> The friendly spirit of England was especially shown in the conduct of the fleets in Manila Bay. The German admiral, Von Diederich, hectored Dewey by unfriendly demonstrations, and would have effected a combination of the European warships to attempt to drive Dewey from the bay or to frustrate his bombardment of Manila, had not the British admiral openly declared his sympathy for the American cause.

When the news of Dewey's victory reached London, American flags were hung in the streets and "The Star Spangled Banner" was played in the theaters and music halls. (p. 589)

A 1920s editorial ("Three Types of Textbook," 1922) included examples of textbook passages that were judged to be excessively pro-British. The author of one of these books was accused of being a British conspirator after he wrote that John Hancock was a smuggler but then failed to make exculpatory remarks about Hancock's patriotism. Another textbook author was assumed to harbor bad faith after he wrote that it was useless to debate which side was correct during the Revolutionary War, because the viewpoints of the United States and Great Britain were irreconcilable. Blanshard (1955) concluded that Britain-centered textbook criticism eventually waned after other types of complaints, such as charges that educational materials were undermining religion, began to attract more publicity. Nonetheless, he indicated that zealous critics, especially those who had tried to expose pro-British textbooks, had been extremely influential in the "great anti-textbook drives" of the 1920s.

Efforts to detect nationalistic biases in textbooks continued throughout the 1920s and 1930s. In many instances, these biases were unconcealed and even calculated. For example, Vannest and Smith (1931) chose as their textbook's frontispiece a World War I Liberty bond poster that depicted a Red Cross nurse with her hands placed on the shoulders of two servicemen. The American flag was behind and supplicant citizens with arms raised surrounded them. In the text itself, the authors' rhetoric complemented this type of artwork. They began the section on World War I by noting that "the United States has always been a world power in the sense that it has stood firmly and squarely for international law" and that "its record in this respect is far better than that of any other nation" (p. 547). In certain cases, textbook biases were so subtle that the authors and publishers may not have been aware of them. Unintentional biases may have been discernible in maps, such as one of those that was used in a textbook by Van Cleef (1937) and that depicted the United States "and its possessions."

At the end of the 1920s, Cook (1927) lamented the nationalism that had prodded textbook authors to write demeaning depictions of immigrants and their ancestors. He cited prejudicial passages about African, Asian, and southern European immigrants. As an example, the following passage is from an American history textbook (Muzzey, 1911):

The Germans, Irish, Swedes, and English are being replaced by the Hungarians, Poles, Russians, Italians, and other peoples of southern and eastern Europe....Their low standards of living tend to reduce wages and their congestion in the slums of the great cities makes breeding places for disease and offers the unscrupulous politician cheap votes with which to debauch the city government....The whole question of immigration is summed up in this: Can we assimilate and mold into citizenship the millions who are coming to our shores, or will they remain an ever-increasing body of aliens, an undigested and indigestible element in our body politic, and a constant menace to our free institutions? (pp. 621–622)

Prejudiced remarks about immigrants were typically accompanied by pictures in which the immigrants were shown hurriedly departing from a homeland port, arriving confused at Ellis Island, or shuffling disorientedly through slums. Needless to say, such pictures did not present a positive image of the immigrants nor their home countries. In the textbook from which the preceding passage was extracted, the author (Muzzey, 1911) included the illustration of the helpless group of individuals depicted in Figure 2.1. To underscore their needs, the immigrants carry their meager belongings in sacks and baskets, and one of the persons is barefoot. The eccentricity of the entire group is further accentuated by distinctive ethnic costumes.

Several years later, Perpiñan (1934) completed a study that revealed extensive biases in educational materials. After analyzing over two hundred social studies textbooks, he concluded that the passages that dealt with the Philippines depicted Spaniards as cruel, Americans as altruistic, and Filipinos as unfit for self-government. Assuming a wider perspective than Perpiñan, Pierce (1934) reported about biases in almost 400 textbooks from different academic disciplines. She judged that the books were "shot through and through with national spirit" and that "glory of service to one's country is emphasized, and American customs, institutions, and ideals are treated as sacrosanct" (p. 119).

Anti-German sentiments were especially abundant in textbooks during this period. Walworth (1938) noted that incidents raised in German textbooks were omitted from American books. Some of these omissions concerned German explanations for the activities of their World War I submarines. For example, German textbooks indicated that their leaders used submarines to deal effectively with hostile merchant ships that had been disguised or with ships from non-combating countries that were secretly carrying enemy munitions. Walworth speculated that the attitudes of 1930s German youths toward other countries were being influenced by information that was found exclusively in their textbooks. After detecting additional biased information that was found only in United States textbooks, Walworth predicted that the students from the two countries would develop hostile attitudes toward each other.

Figure 2.1 Early Twentieth-Century Illustrations of Barefoot and Destitute Immigrants Accompanied Textbook Passages that Demeaned Their Homelands

Parallel Developments in the Textbooks of European Countries

The textbooks of the United States as well as European countries exhibited extreme nationalism in the period between World Wars I and II. The proceedings of the Association of History Teachers of the Middle States and Maryland (1923) cited biased passages from materials used in many countries. Sympathetic to this report, Taft (1925) gave an example of a biased passage about Germany that had appeared in a post–World War I French textbook.

> The German Republic is only a fiction. Only her facade has changed…but we can never forget the evil she has done….Up to this time Germany has never been for France other than a cheat who deceives us; a brute who pillages and kills….The savages on the other side of the Rhine have always menaced us, thus the great lines of history have never been effaced. (p. 93)

Taft also quoted prejudiced passages from French textbooks, one of which concluded that the postwar treaty allowed Clemenceau the pretext to "unchain his hatred and revenge against defeated Germany" and in response "a cry of horror broke from the German people weakened by the hunger blockage" (p. 94). To further illustrate the degree of nationalistic bias in schoolbooks, Taft quoted a passage from a French reading textbook.

> Victor has received a delightful present, an engine and a train of cars. In the midst of his delight he suddenly stops short, frowning and thoughtful. After a moment thus, he seizes his wooden mallet and dashes the toy to pieces at his feet. His astonished and somewhat angered mother is rebuked by the child's tearful exclamation: "Mamma, it is Boche." (p. 94)

Though he thought these European passages were incendiary, Taft concluded that American textbooks were just as provocative.

Harbourt (1931) contrasted textbooks that had been adopted in four countries and that contained information about the entry of the United States into World War I. The following passage was from a 1929 American history textbook.

> The underlying cause of our entering the war was the growing belief that Germany was aiming at World Dominion and that her final triumph would prove a menace to human liberty and civilization. No one could doubt that German victory on the continent of Europe would mean the dismemberment and subjection of France…and the overthrow of the British Empire. (Passage from a 1929 history textbook, quoted by Harbourt, 1931, p. 83)

Harbourt contrasted the preceding passage with the following one from a German textbook published that same year.

> It was of course very probable that the opening of the submarine war would force the United States into the conflict. Before Germany took the last step she surprised the world in December, 1916, by a peace offer which strongly emphasized the victories obtained. The Entente refused the offer in an insulting manner, emphasized rather "Germany's guilt" and demanded reparations and securities. This determined the character of the war as a war of destruction and decided the question of unlimited submarine warfare. (Passage from a 1929 history textbook, quoted by Harbourt, 1931, p. 83)

Like Harbourt and other critics of this period, Scott (1926) had provided extensive, detailed examples of biased passages in European textbooks. However, he stood out from his colleagues when he gave advice about promotion of international reconciliation through the adaptation of reading textbooks. For example, he recommended that stories and poems about other countries be included in basal readers, that foreign languages and literature be promoted in high schools, and that Esperanto be taught in the elementary grades.

Pierce (1929) also documented extensive nationalistic biases in the textbooks of France and Germany. Several years after completing this study, she scolded the entire international community because textbooks "tend to

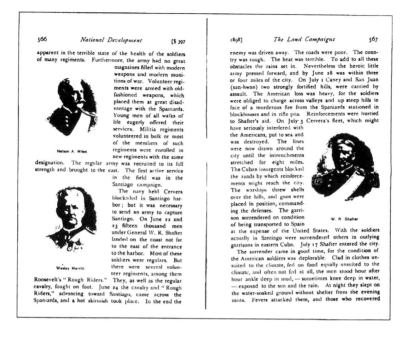

Figure 2.2 Military Leaders Were Prominently Featured
in Early Twentieth-Century History Books

confirm the pessimist in his disbelief that there is possible a worldwide brotherhood through intellectual processes" (1934, p. 120). As examples of the expanding European nationalism, she noted that German Nazis and Italian Fascists were rewriting the history textbooks in their countries. Walworth (1938) made similar observations, warning that unbiased passages about the post–World War I period had been removed from popular German textbooks and replaced with pro-Nazi supplements.

Effect of the 1920s World Amity Movements on Textbooks

Textbooks had been overtly nationalistic before World War I. One indication of this tendency was the frequency with which military leaders were featured in history books. Figure 2.2 contains two pages from a pre–World War I American history textbook (Channing, 1908) on which portraits of three military figures were featured.

Although most textbooks expanded their nationalistic content after World War I, some critics worried that textbook nationalism might be contributing to wars. Harding (1919) sided with this group and recommended that students learn about the "new internationalism" so that they would better understand the merits of cooperative governmental planning. Though he had detected some intolerance to excessive nationalism even before World War I, Harding was optimistic because he thought that educational opposition had increased to unprecedented levels afterwards.

Four years later, Hayes (1923) predicted that World War I would not be the cataclysmic end to war that some had hoped. He adjured educators to prevent another conflict by eliminating nationalism. His attitudes were evident in his detailed, highly editorialized definition of nationalism.

> Nationalism is a proud and boastful habit of mind about one's own nation, accompanied by a supercilious or hostile attitude toward other nations; it admits that individual citizens of one's country may do wrong, but it insists that one's nation is always right. Nationalism is either ignorant and prejudiced or inhuman and jaundiced; in both cases it is a form of mania, a kind of extended and exaggerated egotism and it has easily recognizable symptoms of selfishness and jingoism. Nationalism is artificial and is far from ennobling; in a word, it is *patriotic snobbery.* (p. 250)

Attitudes similar to those of Hayes were apparent in a 1920s report from the Committee on U.S. History Textbooks Used in the U.S. Schools (American Association of University Women, 1929).

> The Word War was a political, economic, and social catastrophe. Ever since its outbreak, hundreds have been asking why it happened, and whether such movements can not be avoided in the future. To answer these questions other hundreds have been delving into the past to find the roots of the war. The conviction has resulted that war, or any great national movement, grows out of national points of view or ways of thinking on public questions, and that these points of view are determined to a great extent by what is taught in the schools; that the school subjects most affecting political, social, and economic points of view are the social studies—economics, sociology, civics, and history—and that the most potent of these is history. (p. 3)

Agreeing that the social studies held a special place in the educational campaign to eliminate war, Kendig-Gill (1923) examined 31 popular history textbooks. She concluded that 25 percent of the content centered on war and that even those books that treated it briefly still glorified it. Only six texts took any notice of the peace movement, and several of these disposed of it in a single sentence. The textbooks failed to illustrate the dark side of war or the limitations of the Versailles Treaty, which she viewed as an unfair settlement calculated to create additional conflict.

Knowlton (1926) advised history teachers about the pro-war as well as anti-war biases in the textbooks written after World War I. Though different books presented distinct political views, all of them were filled with biases. He wrote that even the very best books were "under the spell of this kind of interpretive history" and gave an example using the following textbook passage about Russia after Napoleon's invasion.

> The Tsar had recently made a new friend, the Baroness Krudener. She was a very religious person. "At last," she said, "that black angel, Napoleon, has been overthrown and the time is at hand for the right of the 'White Angel.'" This "White Angel," or "Napoleon of Peace," was to be no other than the Tsar himself for whom the world had long been waiting. (Passage from a post–World War I textbook, quoted by Knowlton, 1926, p. 36)

Because the amity movement was a worldwide initiative, the studies investigating the promotion of war through educational materials were not limited to textbooks from the United States. For example, Lutz (1929) provided details about a 1921 study of German textbooks that had been initiated by the Carnegie Endowment for International Peace. The study had attempted to resolve whether German textbooks facilitated "international conciliation, a democratic spirit, and a proper attitude toward the World War" (p. 273). The report concluded that "in Germany military history was still dominant, that monarchs and generals were still glorified, and that children were still being taught that Germany is God's elected, and that might makes right" (Passage from the Carnegie Endowment for International Peace, quoted by Lutz, 1929, p. 273). The report also predicted that German youths would not respect the League of Nations because of the demeaning fashion in which it was described in their textbooks.

Lutz reported that the History Teachers' Association of Germany had made its own study of warfare in textbooks. However, instead of examining German materials, it had used French, Belgian, English, and American books. After their analysis of these textbooks revealed hostile sentiments toward Germany, the German teachers dismissed the Carnegie study as politically one-sided. Though Lutz was sympathetic to the angry responses from the German teachers, he did admit that the authors of German textbooks had disparaged the League of Nations. Lutz tried to find a middle ground on this topic that could be the basis for eventual, educational cooperation between Germany and its critics.

The League of Nations is not a perfect organization, and German authors do point out its imperfections. They do indicate also that much good is to be expected of it in the future. It would be well, also, to point out the achievements of this organization to date, as well as its shortcomings, but we must not expect history in the schools of any country to be League-of-Nationalized. It is not the function of history to preach any cause, no matter how noble it may be. (p. 278)

Kelsey (1921) had earlier suspected that the treatment of war in German textbooks might have been reviewed unfairly by American critics. At the same time the Carnegie Committee was deliberating, Kelsey had sent German teachers a questionnaire about their attitudes toward international cooperation and democracy. Although their responses indicated distrust of the United States, Kelsey still advised American teachers to be sympathetic toward their German peers, who were attempting to deal with a bitter defeat.

Scott (1926) was also cautious about foreign textbooks that might have been criticized unfairly. Although able to detect biased passages in French materials, he still did not think that they were unilaterally nationalistic. To demonstrate this point, he singled out nationalistic and anti-nationalistic passages within the same French curriculum handbook. One paragraph urged teachers to define the responsibilities of the school in promoting patriotism. However, the very next paragraph adjured teachers to emphasize international friendship and the important role of the League of Nations.

With regard to the League of Nations, Scott (1926) had recommended that all teachers inform their students about its efforts to facilitate international reconciliation and cooperation. He admonished them to provide this information irrespective of whether their textbooks supported or opposed the League. However, the League of Nations was itself an agent for educational reform as well as a classroom topic. Prescott (1930) wrote about educational efforts to promote peace. They were formulated by this organization during the 1920s. He observed that the central message of the League was that international cooperation was the only effective method for handling international problems and promoting peace. He wrote that the League was invariably linked to any investigation of war's educational consequences and concluded defensively that even those who ridiculed the League as Utopian still had to acknowledge its influence on many students.

Prescott had cited a passage from a 1923 resolution by the League which urged the "governments of the States' members to arrange that the children and youth in their respective countries where such teaching is not given be made aware of the existence and aims of the League of Nations and the terms of its Covenant" (League of Nations, quoted by Prescott, 1930, p. 105). A 1924 resolution went a step further, adjuring members about the importance

```
          O U R   N A T I O N ' S   D E V E L O P M E N T

                      Barker - Dodd - Commager

ORGANIZATION:  The material is arranged chronologically and topically.  The
    unit-topical method of presentation enables the student to have a more
    comprehensive and surer understanding of significant movements than can
    be obtained from a chronological treatment.

BALANCE AND EMPHASIS:  More than half of the material presented deals with
    movements and events since 1865.  The study of history in the grammar
    grades makes unnecessary detailed discussions of the early history of
    our country.

    The emphasis is broadly social and economic.  Campaigns and military
    movements of the six wars in which the United States has been engaged
    are briefly treated.

WORLD VIEWS AND UNIT PREVIEWS:  A preview opens each unit and a survey of
    conditions in the world at large during the period, or on the topic
    covered by the Unit, is also given.

STYLE AND VOCABULARY:  This book is written in simple, clear style in a
    language which contains no unusual words or difficult constructions.

OUTLINES:  Each chapter is introduced by a complete outline which helps both
    teachers and students to understand the relative importance and sequence
    of events.

ACTIVITY MATERIAL:  An abundance of usable activity material has been provided.
        (a) Problems for oral or written discussion.
        (b) A wide range of activities requiring some outside reading
            and research.
        (c) Supplementary reading references are abundant.

MAPS AND ILLUSTRATIONS:  46 black and white maps and two end-sheet maps in
    color have been especially designed and drawn for the text.

    140 unusual illustrations, each with a teaching legend, are of real interest.

    The colored full-page inserts offer an unusually attractive selection of
    pictures representing historical movements.

                      List Price - $2.20

            R O W ,   P E T E R S O N   A N D   C O M P A N Y

    New York              Evanston, Illinois          San Francisco
```

Figure 2.3 Advertisement for a 1930s History Textbook Promoting an International Worldview and the Brief Treatment of Wars

of familiarizing "young people throughout the world with the principles and work of the League of Nations, and of training the younger generation to regard international coöperation as the normal method of conducting world affairs" (League of Nations, quoted by Prescott, 1930, pp. 105–106). A 1930 proposal approved by the League focused specifically on educational materials, calling for "the revision of school-books effected with a view to the correction of passages harmful to a mutual understanding of the peoples and to a spirit of international amity" (International Institute of Intellectual Co-operation, 1933, p. 1). After reviewing this and other efforts by the League to reform textbooks, one disgruntled critic responded that "the business of the League is to make history, not to command historians" (Zimmern, 1930). Figure 2.3 (p. 41) contains a mimeographed advertisement that was distributed to teachers with sample copies of a 1930s American history textbook (Barker, Dodd, & Commanger, 1937). The advertisement indicated that the book's emphasis was "broadly social and economic" and that "campaigns and military movements" were only "briefly treated." The book highlighted incidents not only from the United States but "conditions of the world at large."

In the book to which the advertisement in Figure 2.3 (p. 41) referred, the authors (Barker, Dodd, & Commanger, 1937) had indicated their disappointment with the United States' rejection of the League of Nations. They wrote that "if the decision was an error, as many Americans believed, the voters have not yet seen fit to reverse it" but that "nevertheless there was, for a time, a growing tendency toward American cooperation in the activities of the League" (p. 758). In an earlier edition of the same textbook (Barker, Webb, & Dodd, 1928), the authors had included a section titled "should the United States join the League?" Their sentiments were unconcealed in the following, editorialized passage:

> The American people were divided on the question of whether or not the United States should join the League of Nations. President Wilson died in 1924, strong in the faith that the future would carry us into the League. Whether his faith shall be realized nobody knows, but the war taught the Americans that they cannot live to themselves alone, that the United States, as a world power, must bear a part in maintaining the peace of the world. If membership in the League seems the best means of achieving that end, we shall no doubt enter the League some day, and Woodrow Wilson's dream will be realized. (pp. 656–657)

An illustration from a civics textbook by Capen and Melchior (1937) promoted the entry of the United States into the League of Nations. This illustration showed Uncle Sam, his nose in the air, walking away from a multiracial group in which the participants were holding hands. In the passage that accompanied this illustration, the authors pointed out that the League's annual budget "was about $6,150,000—the estimated cost of two hours of the war to the United States in 1918" (p. 545). A large section about the League's achievements followed. In an earlier passage, the authors had listed numerous undesirable consequences of war, one of which was that "patriotism, under the stress of war, becomes infused with enemy hatred" (p. 540).

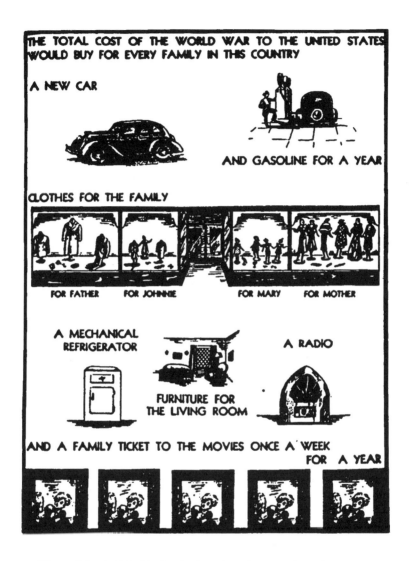

Figure 2.4 A 1930s Textbook Chart that Discouraged War by
Emphasizing Its Unreasonable Costs

Figure 2.4 is an illustration that promoted world peace through
international cooperation. The textbook (Hamm, 1938) in which it was
included emphasized the imprudence of America's entry into World War I.

The caption for the illustration pointed out that, in addition to a war's financial costs, "the damage to biological, cultural, and psychological progress is incalculable (p. 1011).

In another American history textbook, Canfield, Wilder, Paxson, Coulter, and Mead (1938) wrote a chapter that they entitled "the United States Embarks upon a Policy of Imperialism." At the end of this chapter, the authors asked students the following question:

> Kipling referred to the governing of backward peoples as the "white man's burden."
> To what extent do you feel that America's activities in Cuba, Puerto Rico, and the
> Philippines sprang from a desire to assume the "white man's burden?" Give reasons.
> (Canfield, Wilder, Paxson, Coulter, & Mead, 1938, p. 674)

Illustrations and the accompanying text should have revealed the authors' sentiments about the appropriate answer to this question. For within the section about American imperialism, they wrote that the late nineteenth-century interest of the United States in Cuba resulted from "the extension of American industrial enterprise" (p. 654).

Table 2.1 contains nationalistically biased passages from early twentieth-century textbooks. It also contains quotations that refer to the nationalistic biases in them. Indicative of the debates during this era, some of the quotes allege excessive nationalism while others underscore inadequate attention to nationalism.

Attack on Nationalism in Textbooks during the 1930s and World War II

World War II and the period of conflict that preceded it elicited sentiments that were predominantly nationalistic. However, this era also presented a forum for opponents of excessive nationalism. Gestie (1937) judged that international peace was being facilitated by governments that were restricting the nationalistic content in their textbooks. Convinced that world amity could be achieved by eliminating any passages likely to compromise international understanding, she gave specific examples, such as revisions of Austrian and Prussian textbooks after World War I and revisions of Chinese books that had formerly attempted to develop patriotism "with the flame of hatred." She recounted that Finland banned war history in its textbooks, that Norway requested publishers to suppress passages relating to the use of force in international relations, that Rumania withdrew a geography with caustic passages, and that Uruguay revised textbooks that offended its neighbors.

Table 2.1   Textbook Nationalism during the First Half of the Twentieth Century

"For years we have been demanding that the makers of text-books should subordinate purely military incidents to the general course of events." (Standing Committee on Textbooks, 1898)

"Japan is now proud to acknowledge that she owes her recent remarkable progress in western civilization and her present position among Oriental nations in great measure to Perry's success and to the introduction of American inventions and American educational influences." (Passage from an American history textbook, Montgomery, 1905)

"Among the colonizing nations of the world Spain has been notorious for the wretched government of its provinces.... [and] in the interest of humanity the United States was compelled to assert herself." (Passage from a secondary school textbook, Ashley, 1907)

"The historian is seldom called upon nowadays to inspire national hatreds by recalling the cruelties of the other side." (Bushnell, 1911)

"The historian is influenced by the prevailing spirit of his age, and he feeds the spirit of national intolerance to-day as his predecessors fed the flames of religious intolerance in days gone by." (Stephens, 1916)

"The loss of American lives through the persistence of Germany in sinking British and neutral vessels without warning and without placing their passengers and crews in safety was one of the causes of the entrance of our country into the World War in 1917." (Passage from an American history textbook, Burnham, 1920)

"Textbooks lacking in patriotism and filled with foreign propaganda were revealed during the war." (Searson, 1920)

"[German students are studying] history that is tainted and perverted at the source." (Tighe, 1920)

"[The United States invaded Mexico in 1914 because] the United States was unwilling that any other power should enter Mexico, and used its influence for the protection of all non-Mexicans who were in that country." (Passage from a history textbook, Hart, 1921)

"[Germans] were taught to believe that might makes right and that it was the mission of Germany to force her civilization upon the world." (Passage from a 1921 history textbook, quoted by Harbourt, 1931)

"Certain officials are alarmed, alleging that of the history textbooks in use some are pro-English." ("Three Types of Textbook," 1922)

Continued on next page

Table 2.1   (Continued)

"[Text]books have aroused the violent and organized opposition of propagandist organizations, whose members hate everything English." (Turner, 1922)

"German children read: 'Germany made every effort to localize the Austro-Serbian dispute, but the enemy nations openly incited war among their people.'" (Taft, 1925)

"I shall be critical of my government only in so far as I can be constructive." (Passage in a civics textbook, Moore, 1936)

"What may be only an innocent manifestation of national vanity in one's own texts is a source of international peril when indulged in by the schoolbooks of other countries." (Schlesinger, 1938)

"A substantial proportion of the social-science textbooks used in the high schools tend to criticize our form of government and hold in contempt the system of private enterprise." (New York Times, 1940, quoted by Flynn, 1951)

"[Textbooks reveal] no evidence of conscious and perverted antagonism toward Latin America…[and] the errors and inadequacies noted seem to be largely unconscious." (American Council on Education, 1944)

"[Textbooks] tend to give two rather well-defined pictures of the Orient: first, that everything in Asia is alike, no matter where it is found; and second, that anything Oriental is neither so good nor so advanced as its counterpart in Western life." (Burkhardt, 1946)

"[In United States history textbooks,] Canada is infrequently, if ever, mentioned except in connection with controversies." (Hunt, 1947)

"It has long been held that much could be done to improve international friendship by careful attention to what is said and not said in the school textbooks." (Zook, 1948)

Gestie also documented the work of a committee from the League of Nations that had pledged to eliminate confrontational references from educational materials. To facilitate appropriate publications, this committee had assembled an archive of prototypical materials that were either particularly positive or offensive. Because she was a supporter of international alliances to promote educational rapprochement, Gestie illustrated an especially noteworthy proposal intended to help French and German teachers amicably depict controversial World War I incidents. Although the agreement itself was never ratified, the idealistic Gestie judged that even rejection was a positive step since it demonstrated that the two governments were aware of the agreement's premises. Zook (1939) was also Pollyannaish in his search for strategies to promote world peace. He was excited about the benefits from exchanges of students, professors, school administrators, and even educational publications. He also hoped that a committee of historians and teachers would develop principles for global cooperation that might lead to world peace.

Zook was a leader in the global cooperation movement. Nolen (1942) recorded the earlier stages of this movement, concluding that after World War I "the United States had wholeheartedly embraced the World Fellowship movement, and we felt, rightly or wrongly, that if the children of all countries could be real and close and friendly to one another, there could never be another war" (p. 348). One of the ways that educators emphasized the link between school materials and war was by documenting the disproportionate amount of textbook content devoted to war. Levine (1937) determined that 18 percent of the space in popular history textbooks discussed war, but only 22 percent reviewed other equally critical issues. The prevention of conflict, American imperialism, propaganda, and political graft were some of the issues that he thought were important but that had been avoided to make room for discussions of war.

Cole (1939) analyzed the war content in history textbooks published before World War I, when 27 percent of the content was devoted to war. After noting that the war content eventually decreased to less than 16 percent, he estimated that some of this reduction was the result of an increasing curricular emphasis on social and industrial history. However, he judged that the most influential cause of the reduction was increased anti-war attitudes, which had been promoted by peace organizations. As examples, he pointed out that bibliographies of textbooks and school materials that discouraged war had been published by the Carnegie Endowment for International Peace and the National Council for the Prevention of War. The Association for Peace Education and the American Association of University Women had also raised the public's consciousness to the danger of textbooks through research studies that documented the amount of content devoted to war. Cole was personally convinced that textbooks with reduced patriotic content were not only more accurate but that they promoted world peace. Nonetheless, he was aware of popular textbooks that contained large sections about war. Though he disapproved of these, he still felt reassured that his own convictions were becoming generally accepted because even those textbook authors who glorified war tended to concentrate on remote rather than recent wars.

Figure 2.5 (p. 48) is an illustration from a 1930s history text (Coleman & Wesley, 1939) depicting "typical U.S. interference in Central and South

(1) Revolution and disorder come about

(2) This usually leads to breakdown of government and bankruptcy

(3) European invasion is threatened (to protect investments)

(4) The U.S. marines land and restore order

(5) They improve schools, roads, sanitation

(6) National finances are put in order and stability restored

THE STEPS OF TYPICAL U.S. INTERFERENCE IN CENTRAL AND SOUTH AMERICAN AFFAIRS

Figure 2.5 A 1930s Textbook Illustration Depicting "U.S. Interference" in Foreign Affairs

American affairs." At the time this book was written, the United States was already preparing for war. In the final paragraph of the book, the authors reported that the Congress had authorized the expansion of the Navy. Even so, they did not conceal their skepticism for this type of military preparedness when they added that "we hope to remain at peace, and some people believe that a big navy, by discouraging attacks upon us, will help to preserve peace" (p. 623).

The popularity of views about world cooperation diminished during World War II. As an example of the nationalistic materials that prevailed, Faulkner, Kepner, and Bartlett (1941) wrote an early 1940s history book that contained a map illustrating geographical "lines of defense" against totalitarian governments. This map highlighted the strategic importance of outlying naval stations and air bases in areas such as the Philippines, Hawaii, and the Aleutian Islands. The same textbook contained a poster from the League for Human Rights, Freedom, and Democracy. This nationalistic illustration was placed in a chapter about war as a threat to democracy. One of the prophetic units in this chapter was titled "The Outbreak of Another World War Seems to Crush All Hopes for World Peace" (p. 606).

Despite the change in public sentiments toward nationalism, some proponents of world amity held fast to their conviction that education was critical to world peace. Even after the war had escalated, Zook (1944) continued to advise educators to emphasize international cooperation because all countries shared a common destiny. Although such adjurations continued, the pedagogical strategies to facilitate the objectives were not apparent. A report on inter-group relations that originated from a committee of the American Council on Education (National Association of Secondary-School Principals, 1949) provided teachers with anecdotes to illustrate how multinational sensitivity could be developed as a component of the traditional curricula. Zook (1948) thought that amicable international relations would be advanced, even if schools were only to eliminate nationalistic biases from textbooks. From a complementary perspective, Lauwerys (1953) reported about a 1950 United Nations seminar at which the participants volunteered to promote international cooperation by reducing nationalistic textbook bias.

Government Censorship

Skeptical about whether materials highlighting international cooperation would actually deter war, most educators endorsed textbooks tied to patriotism. Most of them also supported efforts to foster national unity through censorship.

Lehmann-Haupt, Wroth, and Silver (1951) chronicled the creation of the U.S. Office of Censorship during this period. Despite the potential authority that this office could have wielded, the agency espoused voluntary self-censorship. Blanshard (1955) used the phrase "enlightened censorship-by-persuasion" to characterize these voluntary efforts. In contrast to such consensus building measures, the only draconian instance of censorship may have been the Soldier Voting Law of 1944, which did place unreasonable restrictions on servicemen. This ambiguous law banned the dissemination of "political argument or political propaganda of any kind designed or calculated to affect the result of any election" (Passage from the Soldier Voting Law, quoted by Blanshard, 1955, p. 119).

Though censorship was not a publicly controversial issue, some educators did protest. To investigate whether censorship and government regulations were necessary, Reynolds (1952) examined nationalistic biases in textbook passages about immigrants. After looking at materials published from 1861 to 1947, he concluded that their general treatment had improved and negative stereotypes had been reduced. He judged that the massive social and political shifts of World War II had significantly influenced these beneficial trends. Because democratic processes were driving textbook improvements, he recommended that professional, political, and government agencies cease coercive censoring.

Although Reynolds expressed confidence in self-censorship, some of the individuals who had supported government-regulated restrictions had done so precisely because they doubted that self-censorship was effective. In an article entitled "Treason in the Textbooks," Armstrong (1940) cited examples from allegedly treacherous textbooks as evidence that self-censorship could not adequately protect patriotism. He extracted the following passage from a Teachers' Guide that accompanied a popular textbook by Howard Rugg.

> The United States is not a land of opportunity for all our people; for one-fifth of the people do not earn any money at all. There are great differences in the standards of living of the different classes of the people. The majority do [sic] not have any real security. (H. Rugg, quoted by Armstrong, 1940, pp. 9, 51)

Figure 2.6, a political cartoon that was included with Armstrong's 1940 article, depicted the insidious influence of subversive textbooks on American youths.

Like Rugg, Hart (1937) was a professor at Columbia University and a controversial author. He wrote an introductory textbook intended for "younger students" intending to enter professional fields. Hart hoped that the book would provide learners with the intellectual concepts that they needed "to plan more wisely for the future" (p. vi). He admitted that "the amount of

Figure 2.6 A 1940s Cartoon about Subversive Textbooks

purely factual information" in his book had been kept to a minimum, but rationalized this absence because "such information is exceedingly changeable, these days, and each student must discover for himself, from day to day, the information that he needs" (p. vi). In a chapter on social health, he observed that democracy had not been realized anywhere, and "certainly not in America" (p. 133). In order to move toward a true democracy, Hart advised that "we shall find ourselves *in conflict* with many antiquated notions and with many 'old rights,' both private and public." Instead of avoiding these confrontations, he assured students that "to *drift* through conflicts is to decay" (p. 134). At the end of this chapter were "suggestions for further studies," one of which challenged students to identify the signs of "social unhealth" and to support these with illustrations from Canada, the United States, and their own

BREADLINES IN OUR LARGE CITIES RESULT FROM PANIC AND DEPRESSION — A PAYMENT ON THE BILL OF MARS

Figure 2.7 A 1930s Textbook Illustration Connecting
American Capitalism and Public Suffering

communities. Figure 2.7 is an illustration from a distinct 1930s history text (Coleman & Wesley, 1939). This textbook was similar to Hart's in conveying a connection between capitalism and the suffering of American citizens.

In his article about subversive educational materials, Armstrong (1940) included a list of offensive books and periodicals. George Counts had written many of these materials. Armstrong revealed that 200,000 copies of a book by Counts had been imported from the Soviet Union for distribution to school libraries. He adjured citizens to search the schools for materials written by Counts and other dangerous authors. He also entreated them to confront guilty publishers because "with an aroused public opinion on their heels, they go farther [to make patriotic revisions] and would refuse in the future to lend themselves to the insidious destruction of American ideals by way of the minds and hearts of American boys and girls" (Armstrong, 1940, p. 72).

Armstrong's supplications to employ publicity to curb seditious books were repeated by other critics during the following decade. A special issue of the *New Republic* ("Special New Republic Report," 1953) listed numerous instances in which political groups had used publicity to restrict publications. One of the articles in this issue (Davidson, 1953) detailed how a Minnesota priest had initiated a voluntary censorship program in 1941 that eventually was transformed into a mandatory ordinance. This ordinance specified that "it shall be unlawful for any persons, firm, company, or corporation to sell, offer for sale, display, display for sale, print, distribute, or offer for distribution, any comic book, magazine, paper, book or other publication within the City of St. Cloud, Minnesota, which said comic book, magazine, paper, book, or other publication prominently features an account of horrors, robberies, murders, arson, assault with caustic chemicals, assault with a deadly weapon, burglary, kidnaping [*sic*], mayhem, rape, theft, voluntary manslaughter, ridicule of law enforcement or parental authority; or are obscene, immoral or lewd; or ridicules any person or persons because of race, creed or color; or advocates un-American or subversive activities" (St. Cloud ordinance, quoted by Davidson, 1953, p. 13).

Influence of the Cold War on Textbooks

Some of the pre–World War II protestors who had been advocating global peace through textbook revision continued their campaign after the war. Nevins (1947) wrote that the fierce controversy about excessive nationalism in textbooks that had begun during the 1920s was still being fought. Despite opposition from political conservatives who opposed any textbook revisions designed to promote international unity, Nevins concluded that the revisionists were triumphing. He advised politically liberal educators who were pining for the League of Nations to turn to UNESCO because it was a vibrant organization that had adopted the educational goals that had been developed originally by the League. Nevins himself strongly endorsed these goals, one of which urged a reduction in the textbook space given to war.

In agreement with Nevins, Burkhardt (1947–1948) identified the presentation of unbiased information about other nations as a critical educational step to international peace. He characterized passages in American textbooks about the Soviet Union as sketchy, poorly balanced, biased, and factually inaccurate. To help make this point, he referred to Pierce's earlier analysis about Russia's depiction in textbooks. In that original analysis, Pierce (1930) had cited examples in which Bolshevist Russia had been described with adjectives such as *barbarous, brutal, despotic, terrorist,* and *dictatorial.* Burkhardt indicated that this biased writing from the 1930s had continued through two subsequent decades.

Both Burkhardt and Nevins had acknowledged that Russia was not the only nation that had been treated unfairly in textbooks. Additionally, Nevins warned that nations other than the United States were culpable for publishing nationalistic texts that served their own interests. He gave as examples that French and German textbooks had taught youths to hate each other and that Japanese and Latin American texts had nurtured anti-American biases. Even though he was sympathetic to the Soviet Union, Counts (1946) admitted that most Russian textbooks presented an incomplete, distorted, and somber picture of the West.

During the Cold War, liberals and conservatives alike excoriated textbooks. In an article that appeared in the *Christian Herald,* Stillwell (1950) traced textbook criticisms to opposing political camps. With regard to a typical accusation from the political right, she wrote that "such a charge is the special delight of a school board member trying to rake up some startling charges with which to enliven his election campaign" (p. 18). After pointing to the specious motives of some conservative critics, she also acknowledged that it was "no secret that there are leftist groups who would if they could smear America and subtly indoctrinate our children with the perversions of Communism or some other 'ism' foreign to our way of life" (p. 18). She concluded that textbook publishers could produce unbiased materials only if citizens protected them from the extremist groups that were exerting pressure from both the political left and right.

Saveth (1952) corroborated that assaults upon textbooks originated from both conservatives and liberals. He warned that groups on the right included "the watchdogs of 100 per cent Americanism" while those on the left comprised "certain racial and religious groups, and some business organizations" (p. 100). He cited examples of the criticism from the political right.

> The textbook publishers cautioned communities at the beginning of the last school term to guard against "whisperings that your child's textbooks are subversive—that they advocate Socialism, Communism, Collectivism, or 'New Dealism.'" Such insinuations, they warned, are harbingers of a broader offensive "which will undermine your confidence in your child's teachers, which will pit neighbor against neighbor and religion against religion." (p. 100)

Bainbridge (1952) concurred with Saveth's opinions about conservative critics. He observed that a small group of Scarsdale, New York, residents had for more than three years charged Communists with infiltrating their school system. He gave examples of other cities in which similar charges had been made, warning that intellectual vigilantism was spreading across the country. Bainbridge himself did not think that school materials were predisposing students toward socialist philosophies and cautioned that the textbook critics were also attacking the United Nations for educational programs that fostered international cooperation.

Writing a year later, Serviss (1953) cited passages from the proceedings of a House of Representatives Select Committee on Lobbying Activities. Members of this committee had observed that textbooks should not be a medium for advancing "obnoxious doctrines." However, committee members also deplored the activities of self-appointed censors whom they compared to Nazis book-burners. Serviss reproduced an editorialized *New York Times* report that had summarized national censorship efforts.

1. A concerted campaign is under way over the country to censor school and college textbooks, reading materials and other visual aids.
2. Voluntary groups are being formed in nearly every state to screen books for "subversive" or un-American statements. These organizations, not accountable to any legal body, are sometimes doing great harm in their communities.
3. Librarians are intimidated by outside pressures in their choice of books and other materials. Unwilling to risk a public controversy, they meekly accept the requests of the self-appointed groups.
4. Several textbooks and other materials have already been removed from school or college libraries and are effectively on "the blacklist."
5. The attacks on the "subversive" school texts appear to be part of a general campaign against public schools and other educational institutions. (Report from the *New York Times*, quoted by Serviss, 1953)

Other 1950s testimonials pointed to a link between Cold War fears and textbook criticism. For example, Mathews (1953) wrote that from 1948 onwards the country was preoccupied with the threats of Communist infiltration of the schools. McMurray and Cronbach (1955) assessed fear of the Soviet Union as one of the social and political forces that most influenced textbooks after World War II.

A 1953 issue of the *New Republic* contained reports about the extensive banning of books thought to be pro-Communist. This issue also included transcripts of proceedings by a senate committee that was attempting to regulate subversive books. The dialogue indicated disagreements between the archconservative Senator Joseph McCarthy and James Conant, the U.S. High Commissioner to Germany. Centered on the usefulness of publicizing government bans on Communist books, the dispute occurred after Conant had requested funding for informational programs.

McCARTHY: I understand that you have no objection to Congressional committees exposing books by Communist authors on the Information bookshelves, and you have no objection to the removal of these books by Communist authors.

CONANT: I certainly would not object to a Congressional committee investigating anything and making recommendations to the Executive Branch on any subject.

McCARTHY: I think we will pin you down to a precedent because you are asking for $21 million, much of which is to be used for an information program. You would not consider bookburning a rather vicious thing, if we insist that you do not have the works of Communists authors on your shelves over there to indoctrinate the German people?

CONANT: May I once again be sure we are using the words "Communist authors" in the same way, Senator.

McCARTHY: By a Communist author I mean a member of the Communist Party.

CONANT: I agree with you that books by members of the Communist Party should not be on the shelves of the American Information Service in Germany.

McCARTHY: And you think they should be exposed and removed from the book shelves?

CONANT: I think they should be removed. I am inclined to think that if they could be removed without too much publicity it would be much the best course.

McCARTHY: In other words, you object to the publicity attendant to exposure?

CONANT: I think in a case of this sort, if it can be done without publicity it would be much better....I regret the public exposure. I think it would have been much better, Senator, if recommendations were made to the Executive Branch and they could have been removed with the minimum amount of publicity.

McCARTHY: Do you realize they were not removed until they publicly exposed them?

CONANT: That would be a question between the Congress and the Executive Branch. ("Capitol Hill," 1953, p. 10)

Table 2.2   Textbook Nationalism during the Second Half of the Twentieth Century

"Under the guise of fighting Communism, self-constituted committees of citizens are attempting—in some cases with notably successful results—to remove from the public schools all aspects of the education program that do not coincide with their personal prejudices [and] textbooks are the chief point of attack." (Bainbridge, 1952)

"Recently, under the spur of clamorous complaints registered by certain '100 per cent American' organizations, a suspicion has been raised in many people's minds that a shockingly large number of textbooks are carriers of 'subversion.'" (Saveth, 1952)

"The Texas Legislature has passed a bill, signed by the governor, requiring as a prerequisite to the purchase of any textbook an oath by the author that he is not and never has been a member of the Communist Party." ("Nation," 1953)

"We will not have these filthy United Nations texts in the schools of this town." (Dialogue from a "documentary novel," Darling, 1954)

"Textbooks on history, geography, government, and all social topics tend to draw the fire of critics [and] even the words 'society' and 'social' arouse suspicion in the minds of extreme individualists who oppose all forms of socialization and socialism." (Good, 1956)

"[United States history textbooks] belittle authentic patriotism and…equate it with the lunatic fringe which consists of crackpots and xenophobes." (Root, 1959)

"Although a few textbooks continue to refer to immigrants in a patronizing way and as outsiders, more accounts reflect a realization that the United States has been strengthened by the richly diversified heritage of our pluralistic society." (Marcus, 1961)

"The world as inhabited by the compilers of high-school history textbooks tends to be black and white, stereotyped, suitable for perpetuating the myths which pass for history." (Noah, Prince, & Riggs, 1962)

"[The state of Texas desires that] the American history courses in the public schools emphasize in the textbooks our glowing and throbbing history of hearts and souls inspired by wonderful American principles and traditions." (Texas House of Representatives, 1961, quoted by Nelson & Roberts, 1963)

"[Passages about the relationship between Britain and the United States in American textbooks tell] the story of a harsh mother and a brave son." (England, 1963)

Continued on next page

Table 2.2   (Continued)

"The difference between American and English textbooks is striking in the authors' prefaces in the American and English textbooks [because] American authors, as a rule, announce that their book's aim is to inculcate love of country and pride in its history." (Krug, 1963)

"[If textbooks were as deficient as critics have alleged,] how did we, so armed, come through the Depression, fight a global war, sunder the atom, and probe the domain of the stars?" (Jennings, 1964)

"There is a lack of evidence that the civics curriculum has a significant effect on the political orientations of the great majority of American high school students." (Langton & Jennings, 1968)

"It is an inescapable function of an American history text that it affects students' attitudes toward their society." (Bragdon, 1969)

"Our [patriotic] heroes are constantly put down and obscure characters put in to prove the [textbook's] author's point." (Norma Gabler, quoted by Hefley, 1976)

"After every war in which America has fought, history textbooks interpreted that war in succeeding generations....[stressing] the necessity of our involvement and...morality." (Griffen & Marciano, 1980)

"Nationalism and the foreign policy of a nation play an important role in influencing the tone and often the actual content of social studies textbooks." (Fleming, 1981)

"Elementary social studies textbooks in the United States are better today than they have ever been before." (Graham, 1986)

"American history and social studies textbooks are the official portraits of the past that adults hand to the next generation." (Sewall, 1987)

Allen Zoll, a leader in the National Council for American Education, became a visible critic of pro-Communist textbooks. A report in *McCall's* magazine (Morse, 1951) contained an interview in which Zoll connected textbooks to Communist encroachment in the United States. He stated that "most teaching and textbooks are Socialistic" and that "the teachers' colleges are implanted with Socialism." He warned that socialist educators were "deliberate saboteurs, and we're in serious danger from them—just as much as from the Communists" (Zoll, quoted by Morse, p. 102). Zoll observed that his organization was pledged to protecting the United States by systematically identifying and exposing subversive textbooks.

Noah, Prince, and Riggs (1962) examined United States history textbooks to ascertain how Communism had been treated. They lamented that politically biased illustrations and the omission of relevant information ensured that students would be "generally left with only one possible interpretation of the rise of communism in the twentieth century: that it is a conspiratorial movement, a world-wide, backstairs palace revolution, moving by stealth, beards, and bombs to accomplish its nefarious purposes" (p. 431). Writing decades later, Elliott (1990) agreed with the many Cold War critics about the impact of information about Communism on the educational materials developed after World War II. For those critics who estimated that information about Communism was represented in an excessively positive fashion, as well as those who judged that Communism had been unfairly vilified, concluded that fear of the Soviet Union during that era had a profound and pervasive effect on education.

Table 2.2 (p. 57) contains quotations from the second half of the twentieth century that referred to the nationalistic biases in textbooks. Many of these quotes reveal how the cold war colored the criticism of textbooks.

Summary

While conservatives disapproved of textbooks that undermined patriotism, liberals castigated those that excessively glorified nationalism. During the domestic crises of the 1930s, the liberal viewpoint attracted its largest audience. This popularity diminished as the public became preoccupied with national security during World War II. Nevertheless, even during this period of unprecedented unity, liberal critics continued to protest about educational materials that discouraged international cooperation. Opposing demands from liberals and conservatives continued to buffet school materials during the Cold War, when each group lobbied to be the exclusive censor of textbook content.

CHAPTER THREE

Textbooks as Propaganda—
The Racial Era

During the 1960s, educators confronted publishers with explicit examples of racially biased textbooks. After the publishers made revisions, many persons acknowledged improvements. However, politically liberal critics still vilified publishers because they thought they were making adaptations to increase profits rather than promote social reform. Conservative critics were also displeased because the formula-like procedures used to make the revisions produced materials that were less stimulating and less challenging to students.

Analyzing Racism in Textbooks

The detection of racism in textbooks had been a nineteenth- as well as twentieth-century issue. Writing about the discussions of racial issues within the history textbooks used in the South, Morgan (1860) indicated that northern authors had eulogized themselves as "irreproachable moralists" while condemning southerners as "immoral reprobates." He added that this pejorative rhetoric was not confined to history texts but was apparent even in the reading and spelling books, which contained disparaging allusions to the South's "peculiar institutions."

Morgan's nineteenth-century condemnation of biased textbooks was repeated often during the twentieth century. However, the alleged victims of bias shifted from southerners to racial minority groups, especially African Americans. A popular nineteenth-century geography textbook (Warren, 1868) contained extremely biased passages about "white people" and "black people."

> The people of the white race cultivate the ground, build fine houses, and live more comfortably than the people of any other race. They have excellent laws, and have many books and schools....In their native country [black people] are very rude, living in miserable huts and obtaining food by hunting and fishing. In our country, many are intelligent and educated people." (pp. 24–25)

Figure 3.1 (p. 62) contains the illustrations that accompanied these passages in Warren's textbook.

Decades after Warren's book had been published, geography textbooks were still depicting African Americans in biased fashions. Tarr and McMurry

Figure 3.1 Racial Stereotypes Were Undisguised in the Text and Illustrations of This Nineteenth-Century Geography Textbook

(1907) wrote that many Africans "have been transported to other lands as slaves, and have there mingled more or less with the other races" but that "in their original home the negroes [*sic*] are savages, or barbarians of the low type" (p. 242). Dryer (1912) wrote that in Africa "men of a somewhat different and lower type were developed" (p. 257). The pictures that accompanied such passages were far from flattering.

Not only African Americans but American Indians were depicted negatively in textbooks. As an example, Figure 3.2 is an illustration of frontier settlers reacting to an Indian attack. The textbook in which it occurred (Cyr, 1899b) was used widely during the early twentieth century.

The illustration in Figure 3.2 was part of a reading textbook. However, American Indians were usually depicted prejudicially in the illustrations and textual passages of other types of textbooks, especially American histories. Fiske (1899) had written in his textbook that their "kind of life tended to make men cruel and revengeful, and the Indians were unsurpassed for cruelty," for "it was their cherished custom to put captives to death with lingering tortures" (p. 8). Ashley (1907) described Indian character with a three-paragraph quotation that concluded with the remark that "he will not learn the arts of civilization and he and his forest must perish together" (p. 14). In the revised

FLORINDA DEFENDS THE HOUSE AGAINST THE INDIANS.

Figure 3.2 Illustration from a Popular 1899 Reading Textbook
about an Indian Attack

edition of another book that was published originally in 1907, McMaster
(1916) wrote an entire chapter about Indians. The chapter contained passages
about religion and social customs and even ended with a section titled "what
we owe to the Indians." Nonetheless, racial bias was evident when McMaster
wrote one-sidedly that Indians "delighted to fight from behind trees, to creep
through the tall grass and fall upon their enemy unawares" and that "the dead
and wounded were scalped" (p. 109). Irrespective of whether such reporting
was accurate, the absence of comparative reports about the suffering that
Indians themselves had endured influenced the attitudes of the students who
used those materials. Nida (1924) included a picture of a huge force of Indians
cruelly murdering soldiers, women, and children. One of the Indians exultantly
waved a scalp over his head. In an accompanying passage about river travel,
Nida noted that the "savages were lurking along the banks, and if a boat came
near the shore or was driven there by the wind, the crew was attacked by an
overwhelming number of red men....[but] the red men had no relish for an
open, even fight" (p. 91). Barker, Webb, and Dodd (1928) wrote about an
incident in which Andrew Jackson killed 800 Indians while losing only 45 of
his own troops. The authors noted brashly that "when the governor of

Tennessee was asked later how Jackson managed to kill so many Indians, he replied: 'Because he knows how to do it'" (p. 309).

Although numerous textbooks contained racially biased passages and illustrations, some materials, such as Channing's early twentieth-century American history textbook (1908), attempted to redress racial stereotypes. In contrast to the custom of using George Washington for the frontispiece, Channing boldly featured a photograph of Abraham Lincoln. A flattering portrait of Harriet Beecher Stowe accompanied a detailed passage about her novel, and Channing noted that "the effect produced by [Stowe's] publication was most important and far-reaching" (p. 438). In a section about "Southern Blunders," he wrote uncompromisingly that during the Restoration period "Southern whites were determined to deprive the freedmen of the rights guaranteed to them by the amendments, and thus to defeat the object of the reconstruction acts" (Channing, 1908, p. 545). In an earlier edition, Channing (1905) observed that "the slaveholders were in a minority in the South, the Southerners were in a minority in the country as a whole, and the South—economically and physically—was hopelessly inferior to the North" (p. 476).

In a revised edition of a book published originally in 1904, Elson (1941) wrote objectively about confrontations between Indians and settlers. He pointed out that Indian acts "were perhaps no more savage and cruel than any other people in the same stage of development" (p. 30). He added that "no massacre by the Indians ever surpassed in fiendish cruelty the Guadenhutten massacre in the Tuscarawas Valley, Ohio, in March, 1782, when ninety-six peaceful, friendly Indians, who had been converted to Christianity, were murdered in cold blood by a band of white men who called themselves the Pennsylvania militia."

By the 1950s, revisionists had begun to correct the racially biased accounts in textbooks. Pooley and Walcott (1942) included a large section about American Indians in their reading textbook. The stories and accompanying illustrations represented the Indians in a flattering light. The frontispiece for this book showed a handsome and confident American Indian youth teaching two Pilgrim teenagers about nature. In a civics textbook, Hughes (1948) wrote that "white men helped themselves to whatever land they wanted, broke treaties with the Indians, and made whole tribes leave their native homes and move hundreds of miles to reservations which the white man probably thought were not worth much" (p. 322). In a later edition of a history textbook that had appeared originally in 1950, Todd and Curti (1961) included an illustration of William Henry Harrison sitting stoically on his horse while his poised troops routed fleeing American Indians. This same picture had appeared in virtually every twentieth-century American history textbook. However, the following caption accompanied it in Todd and Curti's textbook: "The artist has tried to picture the battle at the point where the Indians, after fighting bravely, finally broke and fled" (p. 239). In another example of a history textbook revision, Hofstadter, Miller, and Aaron (1957) wrote that "Indians all along the frontier were tricked into making grant after grant by treaties they ill understood" (p. 171). On the same page, the authors included a map illustrating "areas ceded to the U.S. by Indians." The choice of rhetoric for the map, inconsistent with that in the accompanying text, may have conveyed a distinct impression about the circumstances under which Europeans had become the dominant racial group throughout the eastern states.

Before they could answer questions about which textbooks were biased and which groups were the victims of bias, educators had to agree upon a valid method for detecting biases. More than 60 years after Morgan (1860) had decried northern educational bias, Alexander (1933) discussed a study designed to identify the racial content in textbooks. He hoped that this study, which revealed that racial content could be placed deliberately or incidentally within books, would persuade publishers to develop books that promoted racial understanding.

Other than a casual reference to the intentional and nonintentional origins of bias, Alexander had not elaborated about techniques for detecting bias. However, a year later, Reddick (1934) proposed a simple, analytical procedure for classifying the racial attitudes of textbook authors. He initially searched for racist messages that authors had stated or implied in their books. Racial bias was discernible in many of the materials published during the early 1920s but still used in schools during the early 1930s. The following passage about African Americans occurred in a history textbook (Burnham, 1920) and followed derogatory passages about immigrants from southern and eastern Europe. The African Americans were contrasted with the original European settlers to the United States:

> The European pioneers who developed our country represented the most highly civilized races in the world, and they brought with them the best things in their home lands. The negro [*sic*] slaves who were brought to America in the seventeenth and eighteenth centuries were barbarous pagans who had been captured or stolen by wicked slave-traders in the jungles of Africa. They were not only far beneath their masters in all civilized ways of living but they were divided from them also by a great gulf of race differences which to this day keeps white people and black people from living together upon a footing of perfect equality. (pp. 547–548)

Figure 3.3 Though Illustrations Symbolizing Democracy Occurred Often in Mid-Twentieth-Century American History Textbooks, Racial Diversity Was Uncommon

Figure 3.4 This Illustration of Slaves Working Happily at a Cotton Gin Appeared in Virtually Every American History Textbook for Generations

One geography textbook (Whitbeck, 1922) informed students that persons in the "equatorial lowlands" of Africa and South America "would, of themselves, scarcely rise above barbarism" because "the climate, always sultry and depressing, robs man of ambition" and consequently "thrift and forethought are not necessary to existence, and so are little practiced" (p. 311).

In addition to explicitly racist passages, Reddick (1934) also attempted to detect material that had been omitted from books. In a subsequent example of this type of prejudice, a popular American history textbook (Freeland, Walker, & Williams, 1937) concluded with an entire chapter on "Working Together." However, this chapter did not contain a single reference to racial or ethnic minority groups. This type of omission was equally apparent in illustrations. Though groups of children were represented frequently in reading textbooks, persons from ethnic minorities were rarely included. For example, Figure 3.3 is an illustration from the title page of a 1930s American history textbook (Coleman & Wesley, 1939).

Figure 3.4 contains an illustration that appeared in a 1940s American history textbook (Hicks, 1949). This illustration had been included in numerous American schoolbooks for generations. Accompanying passages

THE PRODUCTS OF AMERICAN INDUSTRY AND INVENTION
HAVE CREATED MARKETS ALL OVER THE WORLD

Figure 3.5 Illustration from a 1930s History Textbook Depicting White Americans
in a Dominant Manner

about the invention of the cotton gin, the picture depicted impoverished
African American slaves happily discharging manual tasks while their well-
dressed, white owners deliberate about business in the background.

Figure 3.5 contains an illustration from a 1930s textbook (Coleman &
Wesley, 1939) and was intended to symbolize the expanding impact of
American businesses on nonindustrialist countries. As with the illustration of
the cotton gin, it depicted white persons in important roles while non-
Caucasians were represented as subservient. The book in which Figure 3.6
occurred was tailored to gain adoptions in southern states. For example, it
labeled the unit on the Civil War as "a family quarrel." It explained the Ku
Klux Klan's hatred and animosity as "results of the war" and characterized the
Klan as an organization that "sought to control the Negroes by playing upon
their ignorance and superstition" (p. 388). The authors added that the Klan
was able to accomplish three goals: "it frightened the Negroes into better
behavior; it made the carpetbaggers more careful; and it showed the nation
that the southern people would not quietly endure outrages" (pp. 389–390).

Courtesy Bettmann Archive. From woodcut by Healy

"MERRY CHRISTMAS!" AN INSTANCE OF THE KINDLIER ASPECT OF SLAVERY

Figure 3.6   Positive Depiction of Slavery in a 1930s History Textbook

Figure 3.6 is another illustrations from this textbook and showed the "kindlier aspect of slavery."

Using his crude, two-stage procedure, Reddick (1934) had felt confident drawing precise conclusions about biases in American history textbooks. His conclusions were substantively different from those that had been reached six decades earlier and in which Morgan had decried the unfair treatment of southern whites.

> The examination of these materials leads to the conclusions that the average American history textbook used in the South violates the traditional pattern in no essential detail. Most of the books in these sixteen States are pro-Southern with a definite sectional bias. The picture presented of the Negro is altogether unfavorable. As a slave he was happy and docile. As a freedman he was shiftless, sometimes vicious, and easily led into corruption. As a freedman his activities have not been worthy of note. (Reddick, 1934, p. 264)

FIG. 84. One of Morocco's native policemen. Today many of the native people of France's empire help her to maintain peace in her colonies. This is just as true of many native people in the British Empire

Figure 3.7 A 1930s Textbook Illustration Positively Depicting Colonial Natives

A decade after Reddick had conducted his study, Hart (1944) investigated racial bias in the textbook accounts of the African and Native Americans who were living in Latin America. To ensure the validity, he assembled a committee of scholars to examine 800 textbooks. Though they did find unwarranted racial assumptions, the committee's members concluded that the recent materials were free of explicit biases and much better than textbooks from 25 years earlier. Figure 3.7 is an example of a relatively early attempt to positively depict persons from racial minority groups. It is an illustration of an African colonial native that appeared in a progressive social studies textbook (Rugg, 1930).

Wilson (1947) examined over 250 popular textbooks. Like Hart, he concluded that most were free of explicit biases. Nonetheless, he used Reddick's procedure and did discern errors of omission. He gave as an example that the achievements of African Americans were either under-represented or ignored. Carpenter (1941) had earlier used Reddick's procedure and also detected errors of omission in the accounts of African Americans. For example, Carpenter listed failures to include information about "the free Negro during the slavery period, the anti-slavery activities of Negroes themselves, early education and achievements, how restrictions incident to the Negro codes affected the lives of both slave and free Negroes, Negroes as soldiers in all of the wars, and Negro self-help" (p. 75).

Saveth (1949) was another educator who pointed to omitted information and one-sided editorializing in textbook passages about African Americans. After examining materials from the late 1930s, he wrote that the textbooks portrayed all African Americans as satisfied slaves. In addition, they dismissed corruption during the Reconstruction period as a consequence of the former slaves' ignorance and credulousness. Saveth's impressions were corroborated by a pamphlet from the National Association for the Advancement of Colored People (1939), which gave numerous examples of racist passages from popular 1930s textbooks. The pamphlet also listed critical information about African Americans that had been omitted from textbooks. As just one example, the authors identified specific African Americans who had revolted against slavery. Alluding to hundreds of additional protests before the emancipation, they pointed out that none of the rebellious slaves nor their revolts had been mentioned in the textbooks. The authors did not conceal their frustration when they observed that to locate "these true stories you will have to hunt far and wide in musty volumes that are kept in a mere scattering of libraries and research centers" and that often "pages which give an unbiased and accurate picture of the Negro's contribution to a particular period have been torn from these volumes" (National Association for the Advancement of Colored People, 1939, p. 10). In a final piece of procedural advice, the pamphlet's authors recommended that textbook biases be analyzed by racially integrated groups that represented complete communities and not just the schools.

A committee of the American Council on Education (1949) published a report on racial relations in teaching materials in which they noted the complexity of analyzing racial bias in educational materials. They wrote that "it involves accuracy of items of fact scattered widely through the textbooks;

it involves locating errors of omission as well as commission; it involves the assumptions and implications of the materials on printed pages" (p. 18). As an example of a passage replete with assumptions and implications, consider the following remarks from a civics textbook (Hughes, 1948):

> For many years, relationships between white and colored seemed to offer problems almost solely in the South. Recently colored people have moved north to work in mills, and some of the same questions have appeared there. In the South, colored people may work for whites as they did in white families in slavery days, but the southern white man thinks that school, churches, railroad cars, and public places of all kinds should offer separate accommodations for white and colored. Colored people have not always agreed about this point. Some of them, of whom Booker T. Washington, perhaps the most famous of all American Negroes since the Civil War, was a representative, feel that the colored man would do best to try to succeed as a colored man and not insist on mingling socially with white people. (p. 317)

The American Council on Education (1949) recommended that teachers answer three questions when trying to detect textbook racism.

1. What do these teaching materials now present to pupils, directly or by implication, about groups and intergroup relations in American life?
2. How good or how bad is the treatment accorded selected topics which are pertinent to intergroup relations as judged by its accuracy, adequacy, and impact in the development of understanding and mutual respect?
3. What constructive suggestions may be made to the authors, publishers, and users of textbooks and courses of study? (p. 18)

Table 3.1 (p. 74) contains early twentieth-century quotations about racially biased textbook passages. The table also contains some of the passages that led to this criticism. The quotations reveal concerns about textbook portrayals of African Americans as well as persons from other racial and ethnic minority groups.

Analyzing Racism after the Civil Rights Era

Two decades after the American Council on Education (1949) had proposed questions for uncovering bias, Kane (1970) agreed that structured guidelines for detecting textbook racism were needed. He endorsed the 1949 questions that had been developed by the American Council on Education as well as the following 1960 criteria designated by the Anti-Defamation League:

1. *Inclusion.* Information about Nazi persecution, Negroes, Jews, or other minority groups should be incorporated in all relevant portions of the respective texts.
2. *Validity.* Accurate statements should clearly present the pertinent information; they should never be misleading or ambiguous.
3. *Balance.* All aspects of the subject—both negative and positive—should be given reasonable attention; overemphasis on any one aspect to the neglect of another should be avoided to prevent distorted impressions.
4. *Comprehensiveness.* The range of human characteristics should be described in reference to any or all groups so as to eliminate the danger of stereotyping according to race, religion, or national origin or ancestry. Such matters as cultural assimilation and diverse factors affecting groups should be included where relevant.
5. *Concreteness.* The material should be primarily factual and objective. Generalizations, editorializing, and platitudes should be avoided.
6. *Unity.* Information about each group that is dealt with, at any one time and place, should be sufficiently concentrated to be meaningful rather than fragmented into scattered passing references.
7. *Realism.* Social evils, such as Nazi genocide of minorities and restrictive immigration, and unsolved problems, including prejudice and discrimination, should receive frank treatment rather than being defended, minimized, or ignored. (Passage from 1960 Anti-Defamation League materials, quoted by Kane, 1970)

A year later, Allen (1971) proffered different procedures for detecting racial bias. He directed teachers to discern the number of African Americans in pictures, the range of the roles for the African Americans mentioned in the textual passages, and the frequency of any degrading references. Writing during the same period, Rosenberg (1972a) developed a set of 20 questions to assess the treatment of minority groups in textbooks. The initial question encouraged teachers to look for evidence of prejudice, stereotypes, or anything that would be offensive to minority groups. Although this first question focused on the inclusion of offensive material, most of the questions asked whether critical material had been omitted. The three questions that followed the initial one illustrated this analytical tact.

[Does this textbook] suggest, by omission or commission, or by over-emphasis, that any racial, religious, or ethnic segment of our population is more or less worthy, more or less capable, more or less important in the mainstream of American life?

[Does it] utilize numerous opportunities for full, fair, accurate, and balanced treatment of minority groups?

[Does it] provide abundant recognition of black people and other minority groups by placing them frequently in positions of leadership and centrality? (p. 22)

Table 3.1   Textbook Racism during the First Half of the Twentieth Century

"When aroused to vengeance [the Indians] appeared to enjoy nothing better than to pillage and burn the homes of the whites, and to murder with special cruelty the women and children." (Passage from an American history textbook, Mowry & Mowry, 1897)

"[The mule] has been employed in the South chiefly because the negro [*sic*] does not understand handling stock and cannot be trusted with horses." (Passage from a 1902 textbook, quoted by Blanshard, 1955)

"Although the rash conduct of Georgia's legislature and governor deserves partial censure [for appropriating Indian land secured by a federal treaty], the people of the state were acting but naturally, when they endeavored to supplant by white settlers the Indians within their borders." (Passage from an American history textbook, Adams, 1909)

"The purpose of the [Ku Klux Klan] was to prevent the negro [*sic*] from voting, to compel him to work at reasonable wages, and to lead a quiet, peaceable life." (Passage from an American history textbook, Forman, 1919)

"We still welcome healthy, honest, industrious, and intelligent members of the white races....[but it was] felt that there ought to be some restriction upon the coming of the yellow races of Asia, whose members did not readily become like our people in the ideas, habits, and ways of living." (Passage from an American history textbook, Burnham, 1920)

"[In South America,] the Negroes and the mestizos or mixed Spanish and Indian stock are generally considered more competent [than the Indians] but cannot be relied upon [for] they work today and loaf tomorrow, which is one reason why tropical Africa and South America play so small a part in the world's business." (Passage from a geography textbook, Huntington, Williams, Brown, & Chase, 1922)

"The Southern slaveholders had come to believe that the system of slave-labor was quite as good for the negroes [*sic*] as it was for the planters....[and] they said the negroes [*sic*] in the South, living in close touch with a highly civilized group of white people, were in a much better condition than they would be as savages in Africa." (Passage from an American history textbook, Gordy, 1925)

"It is just to praise the good deeds of Americans, but sometimes unfair to omit [from textbooks] foreigners who have also benefited America." (American Association of University Women, 1929)

Continued on next page

Table 3.1 (Continued)

"One large publisher...is including in a civics book for use in Southern high schools a chapter which gives interesting and constructive facts about Negroes." (Alexander, 1933)

"The race conscious have glorified their heroes [in textbooks]." (Cole, 1939)

"[Even though they worked hard, the slaves were] a merry race, for they had no responsibility [and] they had a real gift for music and sang at their work." (Passage from a 1930s textbook, quoted by National Association for the Advancement of Colored People, 1939)

"We want the great army of mothers and fathers of this country to know that the very textbooks which their children study in school are often germ carriers of the most vicious propaganda against America's largest minority, the Negro citizen." (White, 1939)

"In 1935 southern educational leaders, including representatives of the state departments of education of all the southern states, unanimously resolved that 'a textbook giving a faithful account of the contribution of the Negro to the life of our country should be prepared and studied in all public schools, white and colored.'" (Carpenter, 1941)

Rosenberg (1972b) protested that too many textbooks omitted persons from racial minority groups, assigned them secondary roles, or showed them in negative situations such as prisons or mental hospitals.

Writing during the same decade, Butterfield, Demos, Grant, Moy, and Perez (1979) developed a checklist for detecting biased materials. They expressed their criteria as a set of "rights of the child in instructional materials."

In textbooks, children have the right to encounter:
1. themselves, equally portrayed by race and sex;
2. themselves, with positive role models, in nonstereotyping roles;
3. themselves and adults of their own race and sex in decision-making and authoritative roles;
4. themselves, in a variety of socioeconomic backgrounds and settings;
5. national and international stories which represent traditional and contemporary cultures in a variety of settings;
6. two or more minority groups interacting within a story;
7. diversity of color within racial groups in the illustrations;
8. illustrations that reflect the growth patterns of children;

9.   more than one language being spoken;
10. a proportionate number of students with handicapping conditions;
11. accurate, active, and positive portrayals of elderly persons; and,
12. folktales representing ethnic groups. (p. 389)

They thought the use of their criteria might help to overcome the token representation of ethnic minorities that had become apparent after the early 1960s. They noted with disdain that token textbook adaptations had incorporated minority children into illustrations, but this had been done so that the pictured minority persons were smaller, sequestered in the rear of pictures, or positioned with their backs to viewers.

Table 3.2 contains several racially biased textbook passages from the second half of the twentieth century. It also contains quotations about the racial biases in textbooks. Many of these quotes exhibit critical reactions to the textbook changes that were made during the civil rights era.

Disputes about Ameliorated Racism in Textbooks

Some critics acknowledged that racial and ethnic textbook bias was being reduced even during the 1930s and 1940s. Progress was manifest during subsequent decades as well. However, positive textbook changes were especially evident during the 1960s, a decade during which educators placed an unprecedented emphasis on racial issues. Even before the midpoint of that decade, Stewart (1964) was heartened when he observed that textbooks were exhibiting an increasing recognition of the contributions of minority groups. Two years later, a report in *Newsweek* ("Integrating the Texts," 1966) acknowledged that not only African Americans but persons from other minority groups were being increasingly recognized in textbooks.

By the end of 1960s, additional reports indicated that progress had been made. Banks (1969) highlighted changes in those books that were published even during the brief period from 1964 to 1968.

> A comparison of books published in 1964 and in 1968 revealed that significant changes had occurred in the frequency of several types of theme units used to discuss the Negro and race relations. Theme units which referred to achievements, violence and conflict, peaceful resistance to discrimination, and deliberate acts of discrimination occurred more frequently in books published in 1968 than in 1964. This finding indicates that textbook authors have responded, to some degree, to the demand for more comprehensive coverage of the black American in textbooks. (pp. 957, 963)

Table 3.2   Textbook Racism during the Second Half of the Twentieth Century

"In general, the slaves on the cotton and sugar plantations in the lower South were more harshly treated than their fellows further north, but there is abundant testimony to show that the cruel master was the exception—not the rule." (Passage from an American history textbook, Hofstadter, Miller, & Aaron, 1957)

"The image of the Negro projected by the authors is that of a dependent, servile creature, who, with the exception of his ability to sing and make music, has contributed only minimally to the development of his country and is incapable of functioning as a responsible person." (National Association for the Advancement of Colored People review of a textbook, quoted in "Schools in Detroit," 1962)

"We do not believe that one authority living in another state should judge the fitness of textbooks selected by well-qualified and intelligent teachers of our state." (Passage from a resolution approved by the Mississippi Education Association, quoted by Nelson & Roberts, 1963)

"For 277 years—from 1685 until 1962—no Negro characters appeared in first-grade basic readers used in American schools." (Whipple, 1964)

"Unlike the traditional reader, in which standardized suburban tots encounter no problem more painful than dealing with a scraped knee, the Skyline [text]books sensitively portray urban realities for children of different ethnic backgrounds." ("Integrating the Texts," 1966)

"Through the use of a multiethnic reader, white children developed markedly more favorable attitudes toward Negroes." (Lichter & Johnson, 1969)

"A critical look at the current textbook splurge in reaching for the urban market reveals, unfortunately, that life in the tenement, in the slum, is really pretty good and pretty much fun for all: Dick and Jane have just gone slumming." (Grambs, 1970)

"The false picture of an all-white America has been changed in most texts through illustrations using integrated subjects." (Kane, 1970)

"[Political pressures from minority groups have produced] the most intensive and detailed revision of textual materials ever undertaken by a free nation." (Joint Committee of the National Education Association and the Association of American Publishers, 1972)

Continued on next page

Table 3.2 (Continued)

"It has been found by numerous researchers that, in general, members of minority groups in this country have either been given superficial or unflattering coverage in social studies textbooks." (Fox & Hess, 1972)

"What may appear to be a multiethnic first grade reading series may, upon closer inspection, contain few significant characters of ethnic background other than white Anglo-Saxon." (Waite, 1972)

"The publishing industry has shown, in recent years, its rapid inclusion of minority group members in pictures and stories." (O'Donnel, 1973)

"Even in the most poorly rated books, illustrations of blacks are no longer created by shading in white people with a black brush." ("Survey of Textbooks," 1973)

"[This book embodies strategies] designed to increase empathy and decrease inclinations toward egocentrism, ethnocentrism, and stereotyping." (Passage from a teachers' guide, quoted by Fitzgerald, 1979)

"Until a couple of decades ago, American history textbooks tended to ignore the cultural pluralism of American society....[but] some observers now think that textbooks are devoting too much space to ethnic and racial minorities." (Glazer & Ueda, 1983)

"When the civil rights movement demanded increased attention for minorities, committees in northern urban school districts responded by choosing textbooks that included minorities in illustrations [and] soon all textbooks followed this practice." (Follett, 1985)

"Researchers concur that there has been a substantial increase in the amount of material about blacks and Hispanics included in civics and history textbooks since the mid-sixties." (Ellington, 1986)

Kane (1970) was gratified that in a single social studies textbook he had been able to locate illustrations of African American scientists, doctors, researchers, pedestrians, policemen, nurses, students, executives, statesmen, and boy scouts, most of them interacting with white peers. However, the positive changes in textbooks were not confined to illustrations. Janis (1970) noted that the recent high-school social studies texts revealed less biased writing about topics such as slavery, the Reconstruction era, and the civil rights movement. He gave the following example of a passage that had appeared in a 1964 textbook.

> Once slaves had been put to work on American plantations they were seldom cruelly treated, since it was to the interest of the master to keep them healthy and contented. They had little protection, however, from the occasional vicious owner.

Janis contrasted the preceding paragraph with the passage substituted in the 1967 edition of that same book.

> The laws of the southern colonies declared the Negroes to be slaves for life...[and] they even forbade masters to teach Negroes to read for fear that they might acquire dangerous ideas. Whereas in the Spanish colonies slaves were obliged to marry and the integrity of the family was protected, in the English plantation colonies slave marriages had no standing in law and children might be sold away from their mothers. Slaves could own no property and had slight legal protection against irresponsible or cruel masters. In brief, Negroes were treated as cattle. Their only protection was that they were such a valuable commodity that it was to the interest of the master to keep them reasonably healthy and reasonably provided with food, clothing, and shelter. (pp. 293–294)

Rosenberg (1972b) recounted that some textbooks had been initially rejected by the Detroit Board of Education because of negative racial content. These books were subsequently revised to eliminate the criticism. Rosenberg quoted a passage written by a senior publishing executive to his Detroit staff after that company's revised books subsequently qualified for adoption. In that memo, the executive complimented the local group for leading the initiative to make revisions that would serve as positive catalysts for the entire textbook industry.

Despite many noticeable revisions, not all textbooks were changed. In fact, even those that had been commended for their improved treatment of African Americans were still criticized for failing to revise depictions of other minority groups such as Spanish Americans and Asian Americans. Kane (1970) worried that even in those instances where African Americans had been represented in textbooks, many critical facts about them were still omitted. Five years before Kane had expressed this concern, Margolis (1965) had also questioned the genuine impact of textbook reform. His attitudes anticipated those that would be displayed by other educators during the next decade.

> It is not the sort of reform calculated to restore courage to the publisher and independence to the writer. It is the reform of committees and consensus, with new author-teams assembling the books and new pressure groups calling the shots. This is not bad; in fact, it will probably improve our textbooks. But neither is it a solution. The only practical solution to the textbook mess, it seems to me, is a strong teacher. (p. 26)

Other critics questioned whether the textbook reforms that had occurred were sufficient. For example, Mayer (1962) had presented cynical accounts about the lack of incentives for publishers to make substantive changes in their textbooks.

> Rand McNally, showing more courage than most firms, printed two versions of a social-studies text, one of them with a picture of a New York chemistry class which showed some Puerto Rican faces at the lab tables (for Northern distribution), the other with a picture of a lily-white chemistry class (for Southern distribution). Most publishers simply avoid any picture of the races together. A Macmillan civics text got into final proof with a picture of an integrated playground; a salesman spotted it and screamed; and Macmillan, with a gesture of rebuke to the editor responsible, remade the book with a different picture. Row, Peterson's American history text, complete through the 1960 election, deals with Southern resistance to the Supreme Court in a single sentence: Many states, believing the ruling of the Supreme Court was an infringement on state authority and on the rights of its citizens, employed legal devices to prevent integration of the public school. (p. 68)

After reviewing passages from history textbooks that were being used in the South, McLaurin (1971) became convinced that the books still portrayed African Americans as emotionally and intellectually inferior to white southerners. Cohen (1970) judged that even those social studies textbooks from which explicit biases had been removed represented only minor improvements. Nichols and Ochoa (1971) were disappointed with revised textbooks that embodied what they dismissed as token changes. After they had compared American history textbooks from 1969 with the editions from 1963, Turner and Dewey (1973) did acknowledge some improvements. For example, they noted only several pictures of African Americans in earlier editions while dozens appeared in the more recent books. However, they also observed some old pictures that had been hastily doctored to make white persons appear darker. As far as the textual material in the two editions, they could detect only insignificant changes. Zimmerman (1975) lamented that textbooks still did not contain enough information about minority groups. He contrasted editions of textbooks published during the early 1960s with those from later in the decade. The percentage of sentences discussing white Americans had decreased from 95.2 to 93.2 percent, while that discussing African Americans had increased from 0.3 to 2.8 percent. At the same time, the references to Asian Americans had decreased from 3 percent to 2.8 percent and the references to American Indians had increased only slightly.

Disputes about Anesthetized Textbooks

Even before the twentieth century, critics had accused textbooks of failing to develop the critical decision-making skills needed immediately in classrooms and later on in a democracy. A nineteenth-century report from the New England History Teachers' Association (Standing Committee on Text-Books, 1898) acknowledged that even at this early date, some critics saw textbooks "in the light of an evil, to be tolerated because of present human weakness, but for deliverance from which one should earnestly pray" (p. 482). These critics demanded that social studies textbooks be removed and that students learn history with primary source materials. The members of the Standing Committee on Text-Books disagreed, advising them to halt their attacks, concentrate on helping the incompetent teachers who abused sound textbooks, and adopt an instructional model in which students learned to read textbooks and supplementary materials with critical eyes.

Responding more than a decade later to accusations that textbooks were failing to challenge students, William Torrey Harris (1914), the U.S. Commissioner of Education, responded that the primary responsibility of learners in the schools was mastery of the information systematically presented in those textbooks. He admitted that "a deep instinct or an unconscious need" did persuade some teachers to rely excessively on textbooks. He argued that the antidote for this problem was not to banish textbooks but to teach students to read them critically. He advised that learners be "taught to assume a critical attitude towards the statements of the book and to test and verify them, or else disprove them by appeal to other authorities or to actual experiments" (p. 317).

Russell (1914a) observed that broad accusations against textbooks should be tempered because textbooks were not homogeneous materials. Convinced that textbooks needed to be classified according to the philosophies of learning that they embodied, he pointed out that some of them were based on the catechetical method, which emphasized thoughtful application of the information from the text. Catechetical materials contained open-ended questions that students answered through paraphrasing. In contrast, books that promoted rote repetition contained questions that required verbatim memorization. Needless to say, proponents of each of these philosophies judged that books based on the alternative approach were at best inadequate but more likely injurious.

Criticism from the 1920s through the 1950s

Hall-Quest (1920) identified five systems for organizing textbooks. These included a theoretical system, a factual system, and a system that blended theory with factual information. He was not particularly sympathetic to any of these. A fourth model incorporated critical reactions to content, but these reactions were exclusively judgments that had been made by a textbook's authors and about which the students simply read. Hall-Quest then reported about another paradigm, one for which he could not conceal his enthusiasm.

> There remains for mention the textbook whose contents have been selected and arranged with the pupils constantly before the author. Their point of view, the range of interests natural to their stage of development, and the fundamentals of social application possible by means of his particular subject—these control his organization and stimulate an easy, clear, attractive style which makes the book what it is intended to be—an introduction to knowledge and a means of stimulating and directing the pupil to obtain, largely by himself, the salient data of the subject. (p. 48)

The American School Citizenship League (1921) sponsored recommendations for the use of history textbooks. The group explained on the inside of the report's cover that its recommendations "proceed upon the educational principle that 'without a problem there is not learning." Not concealing their disdain for catechetical approaches, the group's members added that they wished "the pupil to think instead of merely to memorize, and to reach conclusions suggested by the text, but not actually stated." Their circumspect view of textbooks was discernible when, in a unit about Indians, they advised teachers that "most of the materials on the Indians to be found in any textbook should not be assigned for memorizing, but instead should be read and discussed by the teacher with the class" (p. 25).

Whipple (1929) wrote that textbooks were no longer being designed to elicit memorization but "active response" from students. He did not offer an argument to support this transition but simply remarked that the rationale should be apparent to any intelligent teacher. Highlighting the new features in textbooks that were intended to ensure that information was assimilated rather than memorized, he pointed to workbook activities, laboratory assignments, diagnostic tests, and remedial exercises.

Written during the following decade, a report from the National Education Association (1937) identified several popular philosophies for teaching social studies. At one end of the continuum was a curriculum organized on the basis of the "subject-matter-set-out-to-be-learned." This instructional philosophy was discouraged because it suppressed learner interest and failed to emphasize the relevance of historical information to contemporary social issues. The "subject-matter-set-out-to-be-learned" approach was contrasted with a critical approach that fostered "the intellectual processes indispensable to the function of society, such as: skill in locating sources of information on social questions, skill in using these sources, skill in exploring and stating both sides of controversial questions, skill in selecting and verifying information, and skill in discussing social problems" (p. 193). In a survey highlighted within this report, twice as many teachers indicated their preference for the critical rather than the recapitulative approach.

Thursfield's (1947) sympathy toward textbooks that promoted critical thinking was evident when he directed students to search for "bias, prejudice, exaggeration, propaganda, suppression of evidence, lack of sufficient sources" in both textbooks and nontraditional classroom materials. Thursfield worried that texts with simplified messages, such as those maintaining that the United States had never lost a war, could lead students to form faulty conclusions about history. Several years later, Lauwerys (1953) reported about a United Nations conference at which the participants arrived at this identical conclusion. They recommended that textbooks be written in ways that encouraged students to think critically about the past and realize that the future was not inevitable.

Criticism during the 1960s

A group of politically liberal textbook critics emerged during the 1960s. Proponents for the revision of instructional materials, they became disillusioned when they judged that the revised materials were not advancing the social agenda they championed. A portion of the dialogue about textbooks during the 1960s concerned this criticism.

A proponent of instructional materials that would promote critical skills, Krug (1960) stood out from many contemporary critics because he judged that social studies textbooks were changing in response to the advice of political lobbying groups rather than historians and instructors. He was especially concerned about the failure of textbooks to highlight the controversial basis for many incidents. He warned that textbooks that concealed this crucial dimension did not help students think critically, understand social studies, or prepare for real life problem solving. That same year, Hechinger (1960) also reported that the new generation of textbooks lacked an author's voice and that controversial issues were being artfully presented to placate political partisans. Despite his personal views, he did relate a testimonial from a textbook author who disagreed with him, pointing out that he had never been pressured to modify his rhetoric by timid or politically reactionary editors. This author reasoned that the rhetoric in textbooks had become more cautious not for political reasons but rather because authors and publishers both wished to ensure that their books enjoyed the longest possible market lives.

Mayer (1962) was opposed to any textbook adaptations that were intended to maximize corporate profits. He equated textbook publishers with the venal executives in tobacco corporations and wrote that they had "made a psychological commitment to the publishing of bad books, as cigarette manufacturers have made a commitment to the wholesomeness of smoking" (p. 71). Because Massialas (1963) was also disappointed with textbook authors and publishers, he recommended that students learn social studies with nontraditional materials. In an earlier article (Massialas, 1961), he had urged instructors of social studies courses to use case studies rather than textbooks to teach about controversial but socially relevant issues. Such issues included birth control, divorce, religion, Communism, internationalism, federal aid to education, and medical care for the aged.

Rundell (1965) listed the advantages of social studies instruction that centered about primary historical documents rather than conventional textbooks.

> The method is to present students at all levels with the original source materials used by professional historians and to let the students create their own history. There is obvious merit in this approach, provided that the problems and materials are selected with great care. Students should understand how the historian—or any scholar—goes about his work. Students should experience the same joy of discovery, as the professional historian when a sequence of events falls into place and as a causal relationship becomes apparent. (p. 523)

Since he was personally unenthusiastic about document-centered approach, Rundell urged his teachers to emphasize conventional historical scholarship so that students could stand on "the shoulders of giants."

Elkin (1965) identified a publisher who had developed 25 separate case-study pamphlets for political science. Teachers were expected to purchase only those pamphlets that complemented their students' interests and the goals set in their individual classrooms. Black (1967) reported about experimental passages that were being used to teach American history. Although the federal government and private foundations had subsidized the development of most of this new material, some publishing houses had also made investments. Black described a unit on colonial history.

An experimental section of the Battle of Lexington poses a startlingly simple question: "What happened on April 19, 1775, at Lexington, Massachusetts?" The student quickly learns that the answer is not simple. The youngsters are given six written versions of the battle. They include three accounts composed by English soldiers and three by Americans. The eighth graders are then asked to show where the British and Americans agreed and disagreed, and finally to construct their own versions of what happened. (p. 82)

Also writing about educators who were substituting documents and source materials for social studies textbooks, Cohen (1970) concluded that skepticism about textbooks had created interest in such alternative materials. However, he cautiously reminded critics that the textbook was the cornerstone of classroom learning and asked them to consider the degree to which students might benefit if they were taught to read critically about controversial issues using their textbooks.

Some educators of this era were so disillusioned with textbooks that they did not think even alternative materials could adequately help students develop the critical skills that they required. Like many of their colleagues, Simon and Harmin (1964) had advised teachers to expose students to information about controversial issues. Like many of their colleagues, they castigated textbooks for failing to develop critical skills. However, they went a step further by recommending that students learn about controversial matters through direct experiences. They gave multiple examples of nontraditional activities through which students could acquire advanced knowledge about societal issues.

Increasingly we are seeing young people who understand the significance of non-violent action. Here we see the "marches" and the more recent "sit-ins" and "freedom-rides." Such acts which bear witness to what we believe in are highly meaningful expressions. A group which boycotts the boycotting is to be cherished, too, of course. (p. 165)

Other student activities that they advocated were drafting letters-to-the-editor, sending money to political organizations, attending meetings, recruiting members for politically liberal organizations, and sending messages to legislators. They counseled teachers to prod their students into face-to-face confrontations with any persons who resisted positive social change.

Lichter and Johnson (1969) were also concerned about learners' responses to inadequate materials. Worried especially about racially biased textbooks, they urged teachers to place African American and nonminority children in integrated schools where they would have personal experiences that could dispute any racist passages in their textbooks. However, Lichter and Johnson conceded that this suggestion was somewhat impractical. As a less desirable but more feasible alternative, they recommended the use of books that portrayed African Americans in unbiased fashions.

Criticism beyond the 1960s

Kirst (1984) judged that textbooks had been progressively "dumbed down." To illustrate this point, he contrasted a 1971 history book with a more recent one. The earlier book described the 1906 San Francisco earthquake in a passage that began with the following two paragraphs.

> Just as the sun was rising on the morning of April 18, 1906, the land along the northern part of the San Andreas Fault began to shift. The ground on the west side of the fault moved north. The ground of the east side moved south. Posts that had once stood side by side ended as much as sixteen feet apart.

> Near Santa Cruz, trees five-feet thick were broken in two. Buildings collapsed in cities from Santa Rose in the north to Hollister in the south. Many of the fine new buildings at Stanford University near Palo Alto tumbled to the ground. People were thrown violently off their feet.

Kirst compared the information in the preceding passage with that from a 1980s book in which the information was reduced to a single paragraph.

> San Francisco sits on top of a very long fault called the San Andreas Fault. This fault is more than 1,000 kilometers (650 miles) long. At 5:13 in the morning, April 18, 1906, the San Andreas Fault slipped and shifted. A two-minute earthquake shook San Francisco. Buildings fell apart. Chimneys were knocked over. Water pipes broke. In certain cases, entire buildings fell upon those inside, killing many people.

Kirst concluded that the more recent textbook was less effective as a learning tool because it had lost much of its excitement and interest.

Ravitch and Finn (1987) described a national assessment of historical knowledge among 17-year-olds. Disappointed with the learning reported in the survey, they blamed some of the poor performance on a new generation of history textbooks that was dominating high schools. They criticized these materials for their bland and banal generalizations about families and communities. They also chastised the popular books for somberly reiterating a catechism of information throughout a curriculum that stretched from the elementary through secondary grades. Ravitch and Finn suggested that the recitation of this core information be replaced by a critical investigation of substantive issues that would become more intricate in proportion to children's own maturation. Although they were to be combined with biographies, stories, and documents, effective textbooks could still be crucial for achieving this goal. These effective textbooks would focus on interesting personalities, facilitate role-playing, promote dramatization, encourage the creation of personalized chronologies, highlight critical events, and prod community-based investigations. They concluded that the two most important features of effective textbooks were accurate content and vigorous presentation.

Sewall (1988) also judged that publishers had reduced textbooks' drama and suppressed authors' voices. To illustrate, he presented a passage about the Revolutionary War from a 1940s textbook.

> After a time Captain Jones had command of another ship, the "Bonhomme Richard." It was an old vessel and not very strong. But in it the brave captain began a battle with one of England's fine ships. The cannons on the two ships kept up a steady roar. The masts were broken, and the sails hung in rags above the decks. Many of the men on the "Bonhomme Richard" lay about the deck dead or dying. The two vessels crashed together, and with his own hands, the American captain lashed them together. By this time the American ship had so many cannon-ball holes in its side that it was beginning to sink. The English captain shouted:
>
> "Do you surrender?"
>
> "Surrender? I've just begun to fight," John Paul Jones roared back at him. It was true. The Americans shot so straight and fast that the English sailors dared not stay on the deck of their ship. Their cannons were silent. At last the English captain surrendered. (Passage from a 1947 textbook, quoted by Sewall, 1988, pp. 555–556)

Sewall contrasted this account with one from a recent textbook.

> The greatest American naval officer was John Paul Jones. He was daring. He attacked ships off the British coast. In a famous battle, Jones's ship, the *Bonhomme Richard*, fought the British ship *Serapis*. At one point in the battle Jones's ship was sinking. When asked to give up, Jones answered, "I have not yet begun to fight." He went on to win. (Passage from a 1986 textbook, quoted by Sewall, 1988, p. 556)

O'Brien (1988) also examined passages from textbooks. However, he compared a revised American history textbook with its original edition. Not only was he able to detect changes in writing style and rhetoric, but he documented that the changes had been politically pressured. For example, he reported that the editors had hired consultants who had judged that the older edition was filled with racism, anti-feminism, and elitism. O'Brien, who had been the coauthor of the teachers' manual that had accompanied this textbook, recorded that the authors became furious and argued that the editors were suppressing their right to express opinions and make judgments. In the end, the editorial team prevailed and the authors did make the directed revisions. The following examples indicate the differences between the original and later editions:

First paragraph, original edition: They called themselves "hippies." They said they admired the simple, natural ways of the American Indian—about whom they usually knew nothing at all. There were not many of them, but they made the headlines and offered an interesting spectacle on television.

First paragraph, revised edition: They wanted to look as different as possible from other Americans. They called themselves "hippies" (from the slang expression "hip," meaning knowledgeable, world-wise, "with it").

Second paragraph, original edition: Then some others, aided by young faculty, organized the Students for a Democratic Society (SDS). "Do not bend, spindle, or fold," the warning on computer cards, was one of their favorite slogans. They called for a New Left—a revitalized radical movement to transform the United States. They said they believed in democracy, but they acted like anarchists. They hated what they called "The Establishment." This included the government and nearly all teachers. They blamed their parents and their teachers for the ills of the world. They were unhappy about the Vietnam War and many other things. They showed it by screaming obscene slogans and disrupting classes. They demanded "Student Power."

Second paragraph, revised edition: Hippies often reacted to American life by "dropping out"—by refusing to be part of it. Other students organized in a New Left to transform America. The first active New Left group was the Student Nonviolent Coordinating Committee (SNCC). This was a small group mainly of southern black students. It was founded in 1960 to coordinate student activities, especially sit-ins, for civil rights. SNCC was soon joined in its efforts by members of Students for a Democratic Society. SDS was an arm of an old social-democratic organization named the League for Industrial Democracy. Early in the 1960s SDS broke away from its parent to present a more radical reform program for America. Both SNCC and SDS were born as reform movements, but both soon were to reject reform and turn to anarchism and disruption. (Passages from original and revised editions of a textbook, quoted by O'Brien, 1988, pp. 12–13)

Because the editors warned that Malcolm X had disparaged and linked inappropriately to Che Guevara, the following paragraph about the New Left was eliminated from the revised edition.

One of their favorite movies was "Dr. Strangelove," or "How I learned to Stop Worrying and Love the Bomb," which ended in nuclear explosions. Their favorite heroes, in fact, were "losers" like Malcolm X or Che Guevara, the Cuban Revolutionary who died trying to export revolution to Bolivia. (Passage from the original edition of a textbook, quoted by O'Brien, 1988)

Incidentally, Daniel Boorstin, a popular and respected historian, was one of the authors who wrote the preceding passages. Although he and his coauthor acceded to the advice of their editors, they protested that the editorial style used in some of their original passages actually helped students perceive a critical aspect of all history, namely that it was written by opinionated individuals. O'Brien concluded his report about the revision of Boorstin's book by suggesting that a litmus test for effective textbooks might be that they provide students with something worth knowing. Boorstin's remarks about the importance of critical thinking were similar to the observations that had been made a year earlier by Ravitch and Finn (1987). They were also very much like those made thirty years earlier by Krug (1960) when he observed that publishers and writers who aspired to improve social studies learning might accomplish this by making their textbooks more stimulating and challenging. Peter Wolfe, an editor for a series of 1960s American history materials, agreed that publishers should place less emphasis on the facts of American history and instead encourage students to think like historians (Wolfe, cited by Black, 1967).

Summary

Twentieth-century critics documented textbooks that included negative racial information or that omitted positive racial information. During the civil rights era, many of these biases were eliminated. However, political liberals castigated the revised textbooks for failing to prepare students to deal with societal inequities. This problem was compounded when their conservative opponents were also displeased with the revised materials, which they thought had been "dumbed down" to accommodate liberal ideology. Additionally, the conservatives worried that the newer educational materials had given students the impression that history had been developed by political consensus rather than the systematic modification of controversial inferences.

CHAPTER FOUR

Textbooks as Propaganda— The Gender Era

During the 1970s, critics noted that few females appeared in textbooks, that those who did were depicted in domestic roles, and that materials were replete with sexist language. Concerned about the impact of these materials on female learners, educators demanded revisions. Similar to the changes that they had made to racially biased materials during the preceding decade, 1970s publishers attempted to detect and eliminate gender bias.

Criticism of Gender Stereotypes during the 1970s

Whereas educators in the 1960s had given extraordinary attention to racial textbook biases, many educators of the subsequent decade focused on biases affecting females. Part of a national dialogue about the rights of women, this initiative assumed that gender-biased textbooks could be aggressively adapted. Numerous textbooks from earlier eras throughout the century had revealed discriminatory patterns. For example, in a lavishly illustrated, 588-page history book, Channing (1908) included only five pictures of women—the wives of Alexander Hamilton, John Jay, and John Adams, the daughter of Aaron Burr, and Harriet Beecher Stowe. The wives were not discussed in the accompanying text and the only reference to Burr's daughter was a note that she might have been the heir for a dynasty that Burr had plotted to establish in Mexico. Harriet Beecher Stowe, who was discussed in the text, was the sole female depicted as a significant figure in United States history. A year later, Adams (1909) published an American history textbook with 548 illustrations, not one of which depicted a female.

When women were featured in textbooks, sometimes the pictures were unflattering. For example, one American history textbook author (Burnham, 1920) explained Puritan retribution with an illustration of a woman who had been publicly submerged in a pond. The accompanying caption stated that "the ducking stool was used to punish women accused of scolding or slander."

Hepner and Hepner (1924) had written a civics book during the early 1920s in which they included a chapter on careers. It contained a section titled "many women are working in gainful occupations; but a woman's primary vocation is home-making" (p. 215). They thought that outside-the-home work experience enabled a woman to "realize some of ambitions to be a part of the workaday world, and second, it gives her a breadth of experience which enables her to understand the difficulties involved in earning money, the nervous strain of daily work, and the disadvantages in many fields of endeavor" (p. 215). They added that "in spite of the increasing numbers of women in gainful occupations, woman's primary vocation will probably always be home-making." Harman, Tucker, and Wrench (1926) included a section on "choosing a vocation" in their civics textbook. The initial sentence in this section asked: "Shall I become a doctor a lawyer a mechanic, a merchant, a laborer, a farmer, a teacher, or shall I follow some other line of work?" Immediately below this question was a photograph with the caption "Girls Learning the Art of Sewing." Later in the book they noted that "from time immemorial a girl's special sphere has been the home" but that "within the last twenty years, woman has revolted against this position of being restricted to the home" (p. 510). A decade later, Darling and Greenberg (1937) wrote a civics textbook in which they included a section on homemaking as a career. Although males did share responsibilities for maintaining the family, they emphasized that the mother would be the "probable full-time home-maker." To be successful at this occupation, a woman needed to be "more than a household drudge or social butterfly" (p. 194).

Figure 4.1 depicts a female holding a tree while two males use tools to dispatch more rugged tasks. It appeared in the chapter on citizenship from a post–World War I family life textbook (Calvert, 1932). This illustration reinforced traditional male and female stereotypes. Gender bias is easy to discern in Figure 4.2 (p. 94), which is from the same textbook. It depicts "Father—The Provider and Protector of the Home" and "Mother—The Organizer and Manager of the Home."

In a civics textbook, O'Rourke (1938) reported that at times it was necessary for women to work outside of their homes. He noted that sometimes this decision was the result of choice rather than need. However, he warned students that when a working woman neglected her children or home, then "any financial gain from her work may be more than offset by the bad effects of her absence" (p. 20). This discussion immediately followed information about the increasing divorce rate, which "in many cases" had led to children being separated from each other, sent to live with relatives, or "placed in institutions."

Early and middle twentieth-century textbooks that depicted females positively were also apparent. Many of these textbooks exhibited women in professional careers and leadership positions. As an example, Figure 4.3 (p. 95) contains illustrations that are from a World War I family life textbook (Kinne

Figure 4.1　Illustrations about Citizenship from a 1930s Family Life Textbook

& Cooley, 1917) and that represent careers for "Girls Who Can Go Away to Study." The illustrations highlight opportunities to be an artist, office manager, teacher, tailor, nurse, or physician. Figure 4.4 (p. 100) contains a problem from a "vocational arithmetic" textbook intended for females (Davis, 1920). The author developed this textbook after being unable to find suitable materials for her students at the Milwaukee School of Trades for Girls.

The illustrations in a post–World War I "Patriotic Reader" (Serl & Pelo, 1919) highlighted influential females from American history. Intended to supplement standard textbooks as a means for promoting nationalistic sentiments, these pictures and their accompanying stories depicted females as patriotic figures who had helped develop the nation.

During the 1920s, some textbooks began to expand the references to females. Although they appeared more often than in the texts of previous eras, women were usually shown as subordinates to males. For example, Nida (1924) included a section on "How the Women Dressed" in a unit on Kentucky and Tennessee pioneers. The picture for this section showed an attractive female, accompanied by two children, walking behind a rifle-wielding

Father—The Provider and Protector of the Home.

Mother—The Organizer and Manager of the Home.

Figure 4.2 1930s Family Life Textbook Illustrations

husband who was stalwartly leading them to church. More than a decade before books such as Nida's had begun to appear, Edna Turpin (1911) had written a history book for a major publishing house. Though her book's treatment of females seemed understated even two decades later, she stood

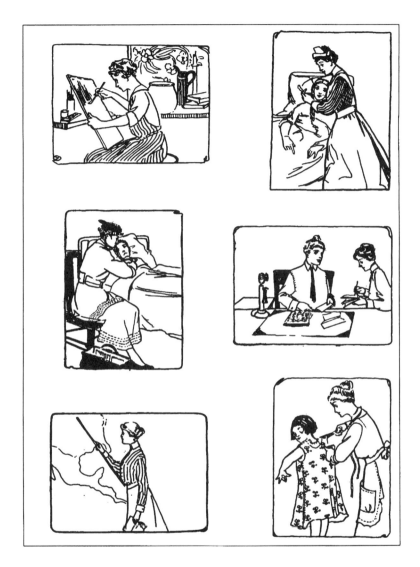

Figure 4.3 World War I Family Life Textbook Illustrating Careers for "Girls Who Can Go Away to Study"

out from contemporary authors as well as most authors of the 1920s. In the section on the colonies, she included pictures of a female spinning thread, dolls of the period, and a young girl modeling the clothing of that day. In the unit on the Revolutionary War, she had a section on women in which she wrote that "women were as brave and patriotic as the men" and that their work "at home did as much for the cause of freedom as the army in the field" (p. 148). She also included a section on the Woman's Christian Temperance Union in which she highlighted the leadership of Frances Willard.

Several decades after Turpin had published her textbook, Ross (1932) published a revision of his sociology textbook in which he indicated that the traditional roles of males and females in American society were changing. He concluded this unit by observing that "thousands of good wives with modern ideas of what is due them will have trouble with well-meaning husbands reared in the old ideas as to the wife's place" (p. 91). Mary Harden coauthored a popular American history textbook (Knowlton & Harden, 1938) that expanded the coverage of women leaders. A section on women in public office concluded with information about governors and members of the House of Representatives as well as a female senator and a cabinet member. The text and illustrations from another American history textbook (Freeland, Walker, & Williams, 1937) called attention to contributions from female leaders. One of this book's authors was also a female.

Although the book by Freeland, Walker, and Williams (1937) highlighted notable American women, this book also included photographs of males in nonstereotypical poses. For example, one picture showed a man putting on lipstick and was titled "performers preparing for television broadcast" (p. 233). An illustration of a male surrounded by children was captioned "a Memphis Tennessee, fireman leads the children in games at a camp established by the Red Cross during a Mississippi flood" (p. 300). The authors developed two entire chapters devoted exclusively to the achievements of female leaders. A section on Amelia Earhart concluded with the observation that "by pluck, courage, and good sportsmanship she has shown that women may be man's equal in doing and daring in the days to come" (p. 310). The following passage introduced a two-page section about Anna Howard Shaw.

> When Anna Howard Shaw was a small girl, she did not like to do the kind of work done by her sisters and mother. Instead, she worked with her brother and father.... Her father and mother often scolded her for "tomboy" ways....At this time it was believed that women did not have minds as good as those of men....As you know, women were not allowed to vote. (Freeland, Walker, & Williams, 1937, p. 294)

At the end of a unit on American women, students were asked the following questions:

1. Name three important changes in the social position of American women during the past one hundred years.
2. Why did the work of Anna Howard Shaw require great courage? Clara Barton?
3. What do you know about the work of the American Red Cross?
4. Why was the work of Jane Addams of such great importance? Do you think she must have been very wise to be able to understand so many different people?
5. When many foreign-born people were coming to the United States they gathered in the cities in "colonies." Why do you suppose they did this? How were they helped by Mary Antin? By Jane Addams?
6. Why do you think the work of Grace Abbott is of great importance to America? (Freeland, Walker, & Williams, 1937, p. 312)

In a history textbook published several years later, Faulkner, Kepner, and Bartlett (1941) included a nineteenth-century cartoon that had mocked women's suffrage. In the accompanying caption, they pointed out that this cartoon currently seemed "ridiculous." Todd and Curti's American history book (1961) contained several sections on women's achievements and on women leaders. A section on "Women in World War II" began with the sentence that "many more women than ever before disregarded the old saying that 'woman's place is in the home'" (p. 759). The illustrations in a high-school German textbook (Fehlau, 1961) showed males in nonstereotypical poses, washing dishes and serving food to a female guest.

Although available, materials that did depict males and females in non-stereotypical roles were not prevalent. Many of the studies conducted during the 1970s specifically examined the representation of females in the older social studies textbooks. For example, Trecker (1971) was concerned that gender stereotypes in high-school history texts had limited the aspirations of females. After examining more than a dozen books published from 1937 through the 1960s, she did detect several instances in which women were featured. However, most of the references were inaccurate or incomplete. Even in those instances where women had been leaders, such as the reform, abolition, and labor movements, only the remarks of men were quoted. Furthermore, she was especially distressed that even recently introduced content, such as pictures and text about African Americans, was limited almost exclusively to males. Without being entirely facetious, she noted that the typical textbook account of women's role in American history could be encapsulated in four sentences.

They held the Seneca Falls Convention on Workmen's Rights in 1848. During the rest of the nineteenth century, they participated in reform movements, chiefly temperance, and were exploited in factories. In 1923 they were given the vote. They joined the

armed forces for the first time during the Second World War and thereafter have
enjoyed the good life in America. (p. 252)

Trecker concluded that substantive textbook changes would transpire not as
a result of actions by publishers but only after pervasive societal changes had
eliminated biases against women.

Not all critics agreed with Trecker that comprehensive, societal reform
was the condition for reducing sexism in textbooks. Convinced that even
simple editorial changes could genuinely promote learning by female students,
O'Donnel (1973) adjured publishers to make gender-centered revisions
comparable to those that they had already made on behalf of racial minorities.
To buttress this advice, he formed a panel with two professors and a dozen
graduate students to evaluate the gender bias in the pictures of social studies
textbooks. He calculated that 73 percent of the pictures contained a central
male figure. He also noted that males were used to illustrate 83 percent of the
occupations and that only one female was associated with a high-salaried
occupation. However, the validity of these findings was compromised when
he conceded that some of the books he had analyzed were outdated editions.

Gender Bias in Reading Materials

During the 1970s, educators showed an interest in the gender biases of reading
materials. These biases were especially discernible in early twentieth-century
reading textbooks. Though these textbooks contained numerous illustrations
of both males and females, they typically portrayed males in active roles with
females watching them. For example, a reading book by Carroll and Brooks
(1906) contained gender-biased illustrations of females observing boys who
were actively playing. The accompanying text directed the students to "see the
boys at play."

Even decades before the 1970s, some concern about gender-biased
reading materials was discernible. Child, Potter, and Levine (1946) had
examined stories in third-grade reading textbooks published after 1930. In
order to evaluate the impact of these stories on children's social and
psychological development, they classified and then separately calculated the
roles of the females and males in the stories. For example, under a category
for "behaviors eliciting knowledge," males were depicted in 74 percent of the
cases. They ruminated about the peculiarity of this statistic.

It is striking that when various kinds of persons who provide information are
considered separately (parents, grandparents, other relatives, children, etc.), it is true

in every case that males predominate among non-related adults who provide information to children—despite the fact that teachers, who are included in this category are always women. Enough unrelated men are brought into the stories as sources of knowledge for the child, so that they outweigh the teachers by two to one. (p. 13)

Thirty years later, Graebner (1972) also studied scholastic reading materials. She examined 554 stories to determine if publishers had changed the depiction of female roles in school readers. After contrasting materials that had been printed in earlier and later editions of textbooks, she did note some superficial changes. For example, she observed that in the new illustrations more women wore slacks, and fewer wore aprons. She also pointed out that anthropomorphic animals, such as female sheep with purses and aprons, had been replaced by asexual, unclothed animals. However, the greatest difference was the number of occupations with which females had become associated. As an example, women who had formerly been shown in only five occupations were later depicted in 26 careers.

Task force members from the National Project on Women in Education (1978) gave details about a study that was based on several thousand stories from the reading texts of 15 different publishers. They concluded that boy-centered stories exceeded girl-centered stories by five to two, that stories with male main characters exceeded those with female main characters by three to one, that male biographies were six times more frequent than female biographies, that male animal stories appeared twice as frequently as female animals stories, and that male folk or fantasy stories were four times more common than female stories. They judged that these materials victimized male as well as female students because the males were being denied opportunities to read about realistic male characters who exhibited fear, sadness, or emotional frustration in reaction to threats and difficulties. Additionally, male students who were drawn to service activities or household tasks were being deprived of male textbook models.

Because children's literature books were employed extensively in the schools as supplements to basal readers or as primary instructional materials, educators began to examine them for gender bias. Nilsen (1971) demonstrated that male-centered themes prevailed within books intended for young readers. In the 58 picture books she examined, only 25 contained illustrations with women. In addition, even these books featured women with aprons. Because primarily females read children's books, Nilsen thought that the materials were reducing the aspirations of females.

Nilsen had assumed that females who were likely to become early readers were the primary audience for children's books. Scores on standardized tests

LESSON XXX

Velvet and silk may be bought with one end cut on the bias and the other on the straight of the goods.

1. Find the cost of material when one end is cut on the bias and the other on the straight.

To find the cost of the material paid for, add the lengths of long and short side and divide this by two.

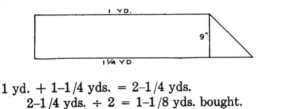

1 yd. + 1–1/4 yds. = 2–1/4 yds.

2–1/4 yds. ÷ 2 = 1–1/8 yds. bought.

Figure 4.4 Problem from a 1920 Vocational Arithmetic Textbook for Females

as well as observations by teachers confirmed this assumption. Decades earlier, Hershey (1954) had reported that females were overrepresented among proficient young readers and underrepresented among problem readers. Though the prevailing explanation assumed gender specific differences in maturational development, Hershey proffered an alternative theory linked to the female-centered content in basal readers.

> There is also a possibility that the pallid content of pre-primers and early readers may have something to do with their trouble. Little boys trying to learn to read in Fairfield witness a lone boy named Tom condemned to play endlessly, and with unnatural control of his manners, with two syrupy girls, Betty and Susan. This frightful life that poor Tom leads is bound up inextricably with the crucial first states of reading. It is not entirely surprising that some boys draw back from the experience. (p. 147)

Hershey's 1950s hypothesis seemed implausible to 1970s textbook critics. The Feminists on Children's Literature Committee (1971), a group of mothers, high school students, and librarians, examined books that had been singled out for their excellence by the American Library Association, the Child Study Association, and the Newbery Award Committee. They concluded that few of the books that had been honored featured female characters, and those

Table 4.1   Criticism of Textbook Gender Bias before 1980

"[In third grade reading textbooks published between 1930 and 1946] only 6 instances of achievement for personal advancement are recorded in girls (as against 79 for boys)." (Child, Potter, & Levine, 1946)

"[In an analysis of the jobs represented in basal reading stories] farming was the central occupation…; fishing ranked second; herding third, and teaching, fourth." (Clyse, 1959)

"Mothers [in reading textbooks] were almost always pictured within the home." (Wargny, 1963)

"The American Library Association bibliography for deprived children…indicates by annotations that the more pastel books will appeal particularly to girls." (Grambs, 1970)

"The linking of a girl's growing up to the abandoning of her 'tomboy' ways is a depressingly frequent theme in [children's] books." (Feminists on Children's Literature Committee, 1971)

"Both men and women [in textbooks] should be shown cooking, cleaning, making household repairs, doing laundry, washing the car, and taking care of children." (Passage from textbook author guidelines, Scott Foresman, 1972)

"Survey of Textbooks Detects Less Bias against Blacks but Little to Please Feminists." (Headline from a report in *The New York Times*, "Survey of Textbooks," 1973)

"Though many women will continue to choose traditional occupations such as homemaker or secretary, women should not be typecast in these roles but shown in a wide variety of professions and trades: as doctors and dentists, not always as nurses; as principals and professors, not always as teachers; as lawyers and judges, not always as social workers; as bank presidents, not always as tellers; as members of Congress, not always as members of the league of Women Voters." (Passage from textbook author guidelines, quoted in "Man," 1974)

"One New York publisher recently received a complaint from Texas because a book submitted on fluid mechanics listed no books by women in the bibliography." (Barber, 1975)

"There is hardly a more controversial issue in education today than sexism." (Harrison & Passero, 1975)

Continued on next page

Table 4.1   (Continued)

"Textbooks still give the impression that independence, initiative, and innovation are traits reserved for males." (Marten & Matlin, 1976)

"This gender stereotyping in textbooks is not self-evident, even to the fair-minded teacher." (Schenck, 1976)

"[Publishers] pictured 50 percent females throughout (one publisher carefully drew a skirt on half of the decorative stick figures in a math book) and removed mothers from the kitchen." (Bowler, 1978)

that did often showcased women who were inappropriate role models. After noting that male characters outnumbered female characters by three to one in the 49 Newbery Award books, they specified the subtle but deleterious social effects.

> Young women who have found it an uphill struggle to identify with the popular female image will recognize it as propaganda—and not simply a natural reflection of life. Unfortunately the girl reader is not yet so experienced. Books that outline a traditional background role for women, praising their domestic accomplishments, their timidity of soul, their gentle appearance and manners, and—at the same time—fail to portray initiative, enterprise, physical prowess, and genuine intellect deliver a powerful message to children of both sexes. Such books are a social poison. (p. 236)

Stewig and Higgs (1973) analyzed 154 picture books and concluded that women were usually portrayed as uninteresting homemakers or professionals in traditionally female occupations. That same year, Wiik (1973) extracted 450 passages from 15 junior high-school literature anthologies. She observed that male authors had written 376 of these selections. Additionally, she counted 440 major male characters but only 88 major female characters. She warned that women would not set high career goals nor succeed financially without changes in the school literature they were reading.

A small group of educators questioned the objectivity of feminist criticism. For example, Fishman (1976) noted that a good portion of this criticism centered on books that were outdated and in some cases unavailable. After contrasting these obsolete textbooks with popular and unbiased materials that the critics had avoided, she warned that feminist critics would not be taken seriously if they made generalizations that were based solely on patently offensive books. Echoing remarks that had been made originally in the 1950s, Zinet (1972) asked whether the high incidence of reading retardation among boys might not be an indication that reading materials discriminated more against males than females.

Sexist Language

Investigations for biased textbook language accompanied the inquiries into illustrations and content. Burr, Dunn, and Farquhar (1972) gave specific examples of terms that embodied outdated assumptions about women.

> Subsuming terms are masculine terms which are commonly believed to include or refer to females as well as males. In fact, however, such terms operate to exclude females. When told that *"Men* by the thousands headed west," or "The average citizen of the United States is proud of *his* heritage," the young reader simply does not form a mental image which includes females. It is of no avail for a parent or teacher to explain that *men* means both *men and women,* or that *he* means both *he and she.* Even an adult is unlikely to picture a group of amicable females when reading about "men of good will." Similarly, when taught that *man*-made improvements have raised America's standard of living, or that a task requires a certain amount of *man*power, a child cannot be expected to develop the concept that females as well as males have participated in the developmental process. (p. 841)

These educators also illustrated sexist quotes from history textbooks. As one example, they highlighted Thomas Paine's remark about the times that try "men's" souls. Because they portrayed females as inconsequential, such quotations were to be cited only to illustrate prejudiced attitudes toward women.

Harrison and Passero (1975) documented the use of sexist language in elementary school textbooks published in the late 1960s and early 1970s. They provided the following samples of biased passages and asked their audience to conjecture about children's impressions.

> When you think of men long ago, you probably think of cavemen. Ancient men used natural caves in the earth for homes…[because] men were then living in the Stone Age.

> Man is a curious animal. He wants to know all about nature. Even since the earliest days, he has looked toward the heavens with wonder.

> Long, long ago men hunted animals and gathered plants for food. They wandered from place to place…then men learned to farm. (pp. 23–24)

As an alternative to this type of prose, Harrison and Passero advocated that the writing demonstrably include females. Additionally, they adjured teachers to change their own language patterns and to call students' attention to any masculine-oriented language that their textbooks contained.

Convinced that textbook biases relegated females to inferior societal strata, Schenck (1976) warned teachers of the damage caused by sexist vocabulary and rhetoric. He developed a taxonomy with eight categories to help educators detect inappropriate language.

- Speciously attributing gender to generic terms.
- Using masculine terms to generalize about a group that includes females.
- Depicting or implying that females are limited to certain abilities, traits, emotions, activities, sex roles, or occupations because they are females.
- Using non-parallel terms when referring to males and females.
- Consistently ignoring or minimizing the existence of females.
- Consistently making reference to the male before the female.
- Using pejorative or girl-watching terms when referring to females.
- Depicting or implying that females are the property of males. (p. 44)

Because more students were entering sexually nontraditional occupations, Schenck thought that textbook publishers were missing an opportunity to support this trend. Nonetheless, he was confident that educators could reverse the negative situation by demanding unbiased teaching materials.

Publishers Respond to Criticism

Aware that their clients were demanding revisions, publishers responded quickly. A monograph on sexism and education from the National Project on Women in Education (1978) reported that, beginning with Scott Foresman in 1972, textbook publishers developed guidelines for detecting and eliminating sexist materials. They summarized the Scott Foresman strategies:

> Using universal rather than masculine terms when referring to all people (substitute humanity, person, people for the generic "man")....avoiding personification of inanimate objects (eliminate the female reference to ships, cars, hurricanes)....avoiding the masculine pronoun to cover both sexes by substituting articles for pronouns, using the passive voice, the plural, or specifying he, or she, she/he.... using neutral rather than masculine occupational terms (firefighter for fireman, police officer for policeman)....using parallel terms like women and men, girls and boys, rather than men and girls to refer to male and female adults....avoiding modifiers of

generic occupational terms (women doctor) or feminine inflections (authoress). (pp. 16–17)

In the actual guidelines, Scott Foresman (1972) had included examples of passages that illustrated sexist language and paired these with revisions. They also provided passages that were demeaning to women or that were based on sexist stereotypes and illustrated how these passages could be rewritten.

McGraw-Hill ("Man," 1974) also published an explicit set of guidelines to ensure that their authors avoided gender bias. In addition to advice about how to characterize females, this manual gave suggestions about the appropriate depiction of males.

> Men should not be shown as constantly subject to the "masculine mystique" in their interests, attitudes, or careers. They should not be made to feel that their self-worth depends entirely upon their income level or the status level of their jobs. They should not be conditioned to believe that a man ought to earn more than a woman or that he ought to be the sole support of a family. (p. 38)

The guidelines gave the example of the following unacceptable sentence, "Henry Harris is a shrewd lawyer, and his wife, Ann, is a striking brunette." This poor sentence was followed by three superior adaptations.

> The Harrises are an attractive couple. Henry is a handsome blond and Ann is a striking brunette.

> The Harrises are highly respected in their fields. Ann is an accomplished musician and Henry is a shrewd lawyer.

> The Harrises are an interesting couple. Henry is a shrewd lawyer and Ann is very active in community (*or* church *or* civic) affairs. ("Man," 1974, p. 104)

Schenck (1976) highlighted sexist conventions in the writing of vocational education textbooks. One of these was "inferior mention," which he defined as consistently referring to the male before the female. Anticipating that some of his examples of sexism might be seen as trivial, he retorted that seemingly insignificant instances of textbook sexism had to be identified and eliminated with the same fervor that had been brought to textbook racism.

Table 4.1 (p. 101) contains quotations about gender-biased textbooks. These remarks were made before 1980. Many of the quotes refer to the textbook changes that were being made during the 1970s in response to accusations of pervasive bias.

Lerner and Rothman (1990) reported that California laws designated mandatory restrictions to reduce gender bias in textbooks. For example, only textbooks with sexually neutral language were eligible for adoption. Because of the volume of books purchased in California, its state laws became the de facto guidelines for the entire publishing industry. Lerner and Rothman summarized the guidelines:

> (1) Illustrations must contain approximately equal proportions of men and women; (2) in the representation of each profession, including parent, men and women must be shown in equal numbers; (3) the contributions of men and women to developments in history or achievements in art or science must appear in equal numbers; (4) mentally and physically active, creative, problem-solving roles, and success or failure in these roles, must be divided evenly between males and females; (5) the number of traditional and non-traditional activities engaged in by characters of both sexes must be approximately even; (6) the gamut of emotions must occur randomly among characters, regardless of gender; and (7) both sexes must be portrayed in nurturing roles with their families. (p. 55)

The preceding examples indicate some of the measures that textbook publishers took to reduce gender biases. However, several critics judged that the publishers eventually made too many concessions. Charging that feminist ideology had become the most noticeable feature of elementary reading materials, Vitz (1986) described changes in the depiction of mothers.

> Hardly a story celebrates motherhood or marriage as a positive goal or as a rich and meaningful way of living. The few with a modest promotherhood emphasis are set in the past or involve ethnic mothers. No story clearly supports motherhood for today's woman. No story shows any woman or girl with a positive relationship to a baby or young child, no story deals with a girl's positive relationship with a doll; no picture shows a girl with a baby or a doll. This absence of any positive portrayals of traditional womanhood is clear evidence of bias. (p. 73)

Vitz also indicated that books involving role reversals, successful females, or leaders in women's movements irritated him.

A year earlier, Davis (1985) had reported that a recent social studies textbook for Houghton Mifflin exhibited calculated strategies for gaining approval from feminists. After examining the revisions to an edition from 17 years earlier, Davis noted that Abigail Adams, who had been mentioned only twice in the original edition, was discussed five times in the new version. She was not only discussed more frequently but characterized as an early champion of equal rights for women. Six years before Davis had published this article, Rout (1979) reported about a critic who was distressed because one textbook

Table 4.2   Criticism of Textbook Gender Bias after 1980

"In California, textbook guardians once complained because one text pictured a small girl struggling to lift a bowling ball." (Dahlin, 1981)

"[In secondary economics textbooks published after 1975] sexist language has, for the most part, been eliminated [and] women with non-traditional careers are often pictured in photographs, highlighted in biographical sketches, and used as examples in the texts." (Hahn & Blankenship, 1983)

"Sex discrimination and sex stereotyping in U.S. History textbooks are a matter for concern in the state of Texas." (Selke, 1983)

"Houghton Mifflin…footnotes the Declaration of Independence in junior-high-school textbooks to declare that the phrase 'all men are created equal' refers to 'all humanity.'" (Davis, 1985)

"A publisher made sure to include a photo of a female truck driver, only to find he had, literally, to stop the presses because of a complaint the female was wearing a pink (i.e., stereotypically feminine) T-shirt." (Marquand, 1985a)

"[Contemporary] stories showing competition, especially physical competition between girls and boys, almost always have the girl winning." (Vitz, 1986)

"[Since] most of America's history is male dominated, in part because in most states women were not allowed to vote in federal elections or hold office until the twentieth century… what then is the nonsexist writer of the American history textbook to do?" (Lerner, Nagai, & Rothman, 1989)

"It appears that picture books did not improve in their treatment of the sexes between 1975 and 1987…[and that female characters] were still underrepresented, especially as central characters, and were given a smaller variety of roles than were male characters." (McDonald, 1989)

"In all subject areas and at all levels publishers have attempted to make sure that women and minority populations are represented through appropriate images of what might have been or should be." (Woodward, 1989)

"Girls appear just as often as boys [in reading textbooks]…and are pictured in a wider range of activities than previously…[but women appear] still not as often as men, or in as wide a range of occupations, even though women biographies outnumber those of men." (Purcell & Stewart, 1990)

"In today's [social studies] texts sexist language does not seem to be a problem, and illustrations of women, in both traditional and unconventional roles, are certainly more plentiful." (Reese, 1994)

Continued on next page

Table 4.2   (Continued)

"Today's textbooks are far less sexist and racist than those of the 1970s, and somewhat more balanced than were texts in 1992." (American Association of University Women, 1999)

contained letters by Abigail Adams in which she discussed everyday matters such as the purchase of drapes. This feminist critic accused the publisher of suppressing Adams's thoughts about substantive issues and emphasizing her domestic interests instead.

Lerner, Nagai, and Rothman (1989) gave numerous examples to demonstrate that the representation of females in popular American history textbooks had expanded. They concluded that although women appeared less frequently than males, the books featured more females who had played incidental roles in major events. Additionally, a panel of judges concluded that critical comments were made about women leaders in only 1 percent of the cases, whereas men were treated critically 29 percent of the time. They actually discerned more pictures of females posed alone and females who had not been depicted in corollary textual passages. Though they admitted that the accomplishments of females in the past had been diminished, hidden, or suppressed because of their political victimization, these authors argued that the extensive examples they were able to cite still amounted only to "filler feminism" rather than genuine attempts to redress gender discrimination.

A report from the American Association of University Women (1992) concluded that efforts to reduce curricular discrimination against females had failed. Rather than providing citations from textbooks, the authors based this conclusion on corollary observations about female students who were being ignored while their male classmates were receiving attention. After examining the original data on which this report had been based and noting that the extra attention to the males had been almost entirely in the form of reprimands, Leo (1999) questioned whether the authors' political enthusiasm had tainted their scholarship.

Table 4.2 (p. 107) contains late twentieth-century quotations about gender-biased textbooks. Some of the quotes confirm, whereas others question, the enduring impact of the adaptations implemented during the 1970s.

Summary

The 1970s textbook critics demonstrated an unprecedented interest in gender bias. The bias for which they searched followed several predictable forms. For example, women were underrepresented in illustrations and passages. When they were included, they were often depicted in domestic roles or traditionally female occupations. The same pattern was apparent in the children's literature books on which many teachers relied. Additional textbook criticism high-lighted sexist language. Faced with protests about the cumulative, deleterious effect of such conventions, publishers made adaptations.

CHAPTER FIVE

Textbooks as Propaganda— The Religious Era

Though they had permeated earlier instructional materials, references to Christianity became less common during the twentieth century. Classroom Bible reading was proposed as the antidote for these omissions. However, the 1920s Scopes "monkey trial" highlighted a distinct curricular threat—academic content antagonistic to theological beliefs. Because they were convinced that even classroom Bible reading could not neutralize such materials, critics promoted the banning of books hostile to religion. Though most twentieth-century religious criticism of textbooks centered about Christianity, some persons did question whether non-Christians had been treated fairly.

Pervasive Religious Sectarianism in Schools

Religion was promoted in those textbooks published before the Civil War. The initial passage of an 1839 reading textbook exemplified this tendency when it stated that "of all books, the Bible is the most interesting and useful to those who will read it attentively" and "it is the only work, that reveals the true story of the creation, and of the first human family; and which clearly unfolds to man his duty and his destiny" (Goodrich, 1839, p. 11).

The McGuffey textbook series, which were sold from the 1830s through the twentieth century, illustrated the integration of religious doctrines with classroom materials. Giordano (2000) reviewed passages from these readers to demonstrate that they had presented nonsectarian moral standards in ways that were compatible with diverse religions. In fact, sectarian adaptability may have been one of the major reasons for the unprecedented and enduring popularity of these textbooks.

Explicit religious content was apparent in the textbooks that were printed at the end of the 1800s and which continued to be used during the early twentieth century. A popular reading series (Cyr, 1899a) contained a biblical psalm that began with the following lines:

> The earth is the Lord's and the fullness thereof;
> The world, and they that dwell therein.
> For he hath founded it upon the seas,
> And established it upon the floods. (p. 33)

when the star made long rays down toward him as he saw it through his tears.

6. Now these rays were so bright, and they seemed to make such a shining way from Earth to Heaven, that when the child went to his solitary bed, he dreamed about the star; and dreamed that, lying where he was, he saw a train of people taken up that sparkling road by angels; and the star, opening, showed him a great world of light, where many more such angels waited to

Figure 5.1 This Religious Passage Appeared in a Reading Textbook Adopted Extensively during the Early Twentieth Century

Figure 5.1 is a page from a reading textbook (Pollard, 1892) that was adopted widely through the early part of the twentieth century. It contains an overtly religious passage.

Russell (1914b) noted that religion had a critical influence on the introduction of history textbooks into early schools because history comple-

Figure 5.2 1930s Textbook Illustrations that Reinforced Moral Lessons

mented the nineteenth-century practice in which children read the Bible while studying famous religious figures. Johnson (1904) reported that the importance of religion in the schools declined as parents, educators, and students became tired of "a steady theological diet." He indicated that sectarian bickering also influenced this decline. Robinson (1930) agreed that feuding between churches during this period had been a primary cause of secularization in the public schools and in fact grew to such proportions that it eventually triggered anti-sectarian legislation.

Throughout the early twentieth century, sectarian diversity and secular values increased. Nonetheless, religion remained in textbooks. Even though they appeared less often in new books, religious passages were still accessible in the older materials. Additionally, many newer textbooks transformed once religious lessons into moral instruction that preserved the same character without referring specifically to Christian doctrines. As an example, Marwick and Smith (1900) wrote a "supplementary reader" that was to be used with social studies textbooks. Supplementary readers with maps, charts, and tables were common in geography and history because many early textbooks lacked these features. However, Marwick and Smith's reader helped students learn about the "moral and ethical" issues that were being omitted from their textbooks. These authors included chapters on traits such as industry, perseverance, honesty, self-denial, and faithfulness. Figure 5.2 (p. 113) contains illustrations from a family life textbook (Calvert, 1932) that also reinforced broad, moral lessons that would be endorsed by religious leaders.

In addition to using older textbooks with explicitly religious passages and newer materials with moral content, students in the schools read and were often instructed with the Bible. Hood (1923) investigated the legal statutes as well as the prevailing practices that were associated with Bible use in public schools. He concluded that although some state laws specifically prohibited religious practices in the schools, Bible reading was frequently excluded. Bible reading was practiced in 19 states that had not enacted specific laws to support it. Hood identified six other states with laws authorizing classroom Bible reading and another six that actually required it.

Table 5.1 contains religiously biased textbook passages from the first half of the twentieth century. It also contains remarks about religiously biased textbooks. These remarks reveal the contentious nature of the debate.

Religion and Science in Textbooks

During the 1920s, educators, legislators, and parents attempted to resolve conflicts between their religious beliefs and public school science curricula. Most of these disputes occurred in the South. In an issue of *Science*, Miller (1922) reported about one state legislative bill that would have revoked any

Table 5.1   Religious Bias in Textbooks from the First Half of the Twentieth Century

"[As a result of the alcoholic temperance movement] thousands were restored to manhood, and incalculable blessings resulted." (Passage from an American history textbook, Mowry & Mowry, 1897)

"[Students], thrilled by our teachings, will drink in our inspiration, and so it will come to pass that our barren schoolrooms will be transfigured into something altogether lovely, into the very scene of Jacob's vision—a ladder reaching up to Heaven, bright rejoicing angels going up and down the steps of it, and at the top thereof the voice of God Himself." (Joel Dorman Steele, textbook author, 1900)

"That the new [third and fourth century AD, Christian-dominated] society should have *feared* both the charm and the contamination of the old pagan poetry it is possible for us to understand; *contempt* for pagan literature and science had less excuse, and savored more of ignorance and bigotry." (Passage from a history textbook, West, 1902)

"Some races, as the negores [*sic*], believe in witchcraft; and among them the witch doctor is sometimes more powerful than the ruler himself...[and] so far as the idea of God is concerned, if these people have any conception of Him, it is of the crudest kind." (Passage from a geography textbook, Tarr & McMurry, 1907)

"In the Hancock school in Boston there were over 1000 Hebrew and Italian children and only 80 Americans." (Passage from an American history textbook, Muzzey, 1911)

"One of the arguments in support of slavery was found in the fact that in both the Old and New Testament human bondage was fully recognized and nowhere condemned [and] this was a powerful argument in the minds of most slaveholders, for they regarded the Bible as the supreme authority on all moral questions." (Passage from an American history textbook, Forman, 1919)

"The keen, persistent, economical and businesslike qualities of the Jews...are well known." (Passage from a geography textbook, Huntington, Williams, Brown, & Chase, 1922)

"In our time, as in all times, superficial people say disparaging things about religion." (Passage from a sociology textbook, Hart, 1924)

"Patrons of School District 18, Jewell County [Kansas]...voted 14 to 5 to order a set of 'The Book of Knowledge' burned...[because] the books were said to contain a thorough discussion of the theory of evolution." ("Battle over Evolution," 1925)

"[Teachers who are evaluating textbooks should assure that] there is no ranting against anything like 'evolution.'" (Andrews, 1926)

Continued on next page

Table 5.1   (Continued)

"[The 1917 Literacy Test Law] prohibits the admission of any alien between the ages of 16 and 55 who cannot read and fairly well interpret a selection of forty words in English or in some other language, usually taken from the Bible." (Passage from a civics textbook, Harman, Tucker, & Wrench, 1926)

"[The textbook] is a guide to the path that is straight and narrow…[and] it is a weapon of defense against the forces of darkness in the jungles of ignorance." (Swift, 1927)

"[Robert E.] Lee has become the embodiment of one of the world's ideals, that of the soldier, the Christian, and the gentleman." (Passage from a reading textbook, Condon, 1928)

"[Religion is important not because] of what one believes, or of what church or creed one follows…[but rather because] everyone should have the help which comes to him who worships God according to his own conscience." (Passage from a civics textbook, Broome & Adams, 1935)

"In our own country, though some sincerely deplore a seeming decline of interest in the church and religious activities, there is no hostility on the part of the government to any religious group." (Passage from a civics textbook, Hughes, 1948)

school's accreditation and imposed a fine as high as $5000 if the instructors taught about atheism, agnosticism, Darwin, or evolution. A month later, the editors of the same journal ("Proposed Legislation," 1922) reported that the Kentucky House of Representatives had almost passed a law forbidding instruction about evolution. The bill was defeated despite an impassioned plea in which the sponsor claimed that information about evolution had shattered his own son's faith. This report also noted that South Carolina had already enacted laws to restrict teaching about evolution.

The 1925 Scopes trial focused national attention on information about evolution in the schools. John Scopes, a high-school teacher from Tennessee, was assisted by a high profile defense team hired by the American Civil Liberties Union. The team tried to discredit the anti-evolution law because it assumed that all citizens believed that the Bible should be interpreted literally (Hays, 1925). The team also argued that scientific information about evolution was quite reconcilable with symbolical interpretations of the Bible. Despite his lawyers' carefully crafted logic, Scopes lost his court case and eventually his appeal. A report in the *Christian Century* ("Is This the End," 1927) noted that the Tennessee Supreme Court upheld the constitutionality of the law under which Scopes was convicted but remanded his case to the lower court only because a fine had been erroneously assessed. The publicity director of the American Civil Liberties Union (Allen, 1926) wrote that the trial left the liberals who had lost the actual court contest feeling that they still had prevailed because of the sympathetic publicity the incident created.

Despite these smug convictions by liberals, state legislatures and boards of education enacted subsequent regulations that complicated teaching about evolution. As an example, the governor of Tennessee threatened teachers with dismissal and prosecution if they did not delete all references to evolution in their school materials ("Anti-Evolution Law," 1926). He also prohibited the purchase of any new textbooks containing information about evolution. Though Scopes was one of the few persons prosecuted, Beale (1936) judged that fear of reprisal had effectively silenced many teachers in the South and in rural, northern communities. The 37 anti-evolution bills introduced in 20 state legislatures between 1921 and 1929 reinforced the prudence of this silence.

Not all states opposed the teaching of evolution. For example, a California textbook adoption committee had concluded that information about evolution should be a component of every biology textbook ("Evolution in Education," 1925). Despite supportive actions by some California communities, Allen (1926), who was associated with the American Civil Liberties Union, was disappointed because the cumulative effect of most local textbook decisions had made California the western state with the "greatest number of gags" on evolution instruction.

Fears about evolution instruction that developed during the 1920s never completely disappeared. Beale (1936) reported that many 1930s teachers were forbidden from using any textbook chapters on evolution. Nelkin (1976) observed that not only chapters on evolution but even the words *evolution* and *Darwin* were omitted from many 1930s textbooks. Gould (1999) highlighted the changes in biology textbooks by contrasting a 1950s edition with an earlier version of the same book.

> *Modern Biology*, by Moon, Mann, and Otto, dominated the market and taught more than half of America's high school students. Evolution occupies only 18 of the book's 662 pages—as chapter 58 out of 60. (Many readers, remembering the realities of high school, will immediately know that most classes never got to this chapter at all.) Moreover, the text never mentions the dreaded "E" word, and refers to Darwin's theory as "the hypothesis of racial development." But the first edition of this textbook, published in 1921, before the Scopes trial, featured Darwin on the frontispiece (my 1956 version substitutes a crowd of industrious beavers for the most celebrated of all naturalists), and includes several chapters treating evolution as both a proven fact and the primary organizing theme for all biological sciences. (p. 139)

After examining biology textbooks and their revisions, Skoog (1984) observed a gradual increase in the information about evolution from 1930 through 1950. Though information about evolution was apparent in the materials developed by large textbook publishers during this era, they used different strategies to present it. For example, Houghton Mifflin published a text (Fitzpatrick & Horton, 1935) that included a photograph of Darwin and factual information about evolution. However, it attempted to diffuse the controversial nature of evolutionary theory by linking it to Aristotle, Lucretius, and other Western intellectuals. Macmillan's biology book (Mavor, 1937) also recapitulated key information about Darwin and evolution. Unlike Houghton Mifflin's book, Macmillan's author boldly asserted that "on the whole it may be said that the logic of Darwin's reasoning and the army of facts which he brought to support it have withstood seventy-five years of bitter and violent criticism" (p. 675). Scott Foresman was another major publisher that included essential information about evolution in its biology textbook (Pieper, Beauchamp, & Frank, 1936). Though the authors wrote in a teacher's preface that historical and biographical content had been incorporated to arouse student interest, they avoided all references to Darwin. Furthermore, they substituted the term *environmental adaptation* for *evolution* throughout the book. Twelve years later, Scott Foresman published another biology textbook (Beauchamp, Williams, & Blough, 1948). Beauchamp, one of the authors of the 1936 book, teamed up with two new authors to write the 1948 textbook that still avoided the term *evolution* by substituting *biological change* and *biological development*.

Though it depicted the concept of evolution, a 1930s biology teacher's manual (Pieper, Beauchamp, & Frank, 1934) omitted terms such as *evolution* and *natural selection*. Figure 5.3 is a chart from a later textbook that also depicted evolutionary concepts using euphemisms rather than controversial terms (Beauchamp, Williams, & Blough, 1948).

Although increased information about evolution appeared in second-half-of-the-century textbooks, regressions did occur. In the fifth edition of a textbook published originally in 1939, Beaver (1958) listed five theories of evolution. In addition to four scientific explanations, he described one based on special creation:

> The traditional theory of evolution which is adhered to by many people, particularly those with a religious background, is simply that which holds all matter to have been originally brought into being by the Creator. This matter was so endowed that it has been able to develop along evolutionary lines to the present. (p. 685)

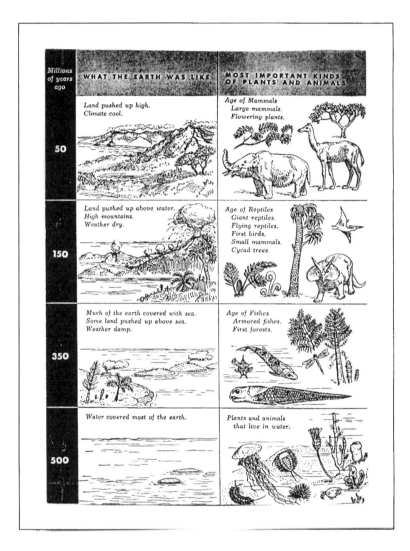

Figure 5.3 A Chart from a 1948 Biology Textbook that Substituted the Terms "Change" and "Development" for Evolution

Skoog (1984) documented erosion in the coverage given to evolution in high-school biology textbooks during the two and a half decades following 1960. As one illustration, he reported that four of the five textbooks that he examined from the 1980s listed special creation as a possible explanation for the origin of life. More than a decade later, Zoll (1999) reported continuing controversy about evolution in science textbooks.

Continued Criticism about the Omission of Religion from Textbooks

Sherwood (1936) had included extensive information about the relationship of church and citizenship in his civics textbook. He presented quotations from government proceedings and from historical documents that struck him as "proof that America believes in God." However, few other textbooks included fervid testimonials about the importance of religion. As a consequence, some critics turned their attention away from books with antagonistic scientific content and refocused it on materials that omitted religious information.

Ross (1932) wrote a sociology textbook in which he not only omitted information about religion but encouraged students to "not flaunt the peculiarities or claims of your religion in the faces of those of other faiths" (p. 312). Other pieces of advice were equally controversial, such as "never try to get your fellow churchman into office for no other reason than that he is your fellow churchman" and "allow no one to dictate to you from the pulpit how you shall vote." Broome and Adams (1935) wrote a civics book in which they included a short section on religion. However, they began by admitting that the church was "a social institution which we have not treated in detail in this book" (p. 380). They explained that its omission was necessary because of "the practical difficulty of treating the subject in such a way as to avoid giving offense." A year later, Moore (1936) made a single reference to religion in his 495-page civics textbook. In a section about "living a wholesome life," he defined religion simply as another opportunity for identifying a "way of life." He added that "putting aside religious difference of which there are quite too many for our good and happiness, we may say that each person should have a plan of wholesome living" (p. 33). Darling and Greenberg (1937) acknowledged that religion was one of two pillars on which government rested. However, they described religion anthropologically as a custom that developed after the primitive savage "started to worship these things that he could not understand or which he greatly feared."

Some publishers reacted to accusations that religion had been omitted from textbooks by printing special materials for sectarian groups. Because Catholics maintained an extensive parochial school system, they became targets for this marketing. In several cases, standard textbooks were adapted into special Catholic editions. For example, the works of authors whom Catholics found offensive were deleted from literature anthologies, and writings by Catholic authors were substituted. In other cases, entirely new books were created. Ostheimer and Delaney (1945) developed a civics book that was part of a series of Catholic social studies materials. They explained that their book's goal was to teach students about social issues in ways that were "guided and strengthened by clear Catholic convictions." Their book included an entire chapter on the interface between Catholicism and government.

Wilson (1947) reviewed textbooks published after World War II and concluded that information about religious groups was sparse. When it was included, it was usually incomplete, as illustrated by the partial, noncontextual depictions of Jews, the Inquisition, or Protestant evangelical movements. Shortly afterward, Pflug (1955) tried to resolve this issue empirically by searching for textbook references to God, the Bible, religion, church, prayer, and life after death. He concluded that textbooks, especially those used in the higher grades, did contain religious content. However, he qualified this with the observation that the religious content was drawn almost exclusively from older eras.

Conservative groups such as the Daughters of the American Revolution regularly reviewed textbooks to see if religious topics were being covered. Nelson and Roberts (1963) cited a publication from this group that objected to 175 textbooks because of seven general reasons, the first of which was the "wary" treatment of the Christian heritage. Price (1966) agreed with the conservative groups that many textbooks did not cover religion. However, he defended the publishers who had omitted it because of its irrelevance to most school topics, its abstraction, or the difficulty of locating material acceptable to both Christians and non-Christians.

In the 1970s, a group of West Virginians judged that local textbooks either omitted or challenged the Christian heritage. They requested their school board to prohibit any books that confronted several of their beliefs, one of which was "belief in a Supernatural Being or a power beyond ourselves or a power beyond our comprehension" (Passage from a 12,000 signature petition that had been presented to the Kanawha County School Board, quoted by Hefley, 1976). The petition also asked the board to ban school materials promoting agnosticism or nihilism. Hillocks (1978) recounted some of the events that ensued when the school board did not implement the petition.

On the two days after Labor Day 1974, Kanawha County, West Virginia erupted into the national media with what was to be the most prolonged, intense, and violent textbook protest this country has ever witnessed. Inflamed over language arts books which had been adopted the previous spring, protesters began a boycott on the first day of school which kept thousands of students out of the county's public school—many for the full school year. On the second day, nearly all coal miners in Kanawha County, and many in neighboring Boone and Fayette Counties, refused to cross picket lines set up by the protesters. As the controversy gained momentum, there were shootings, strikes against other industries, threats against the lives and families of "probook" and "anti-book" people alike, fire bombings and dynamiting of school property, and dozens of arrests. (p. 632)

The county's school board eventually adopted a policy that allowed students or their parents to avoid any textbooks that were incompatible with their religious beliefs.

Mel and Normal Gabler came to West Virginia during this dispute. In a report about their visit, Hefley (1976) indicated that these two textbook critics told large crowds that unregulated textbooks led to intellectual suicide. In an editorial that was published afterwards, the couple (Gabler & Gabler, 1982) explained that their textbook campaign was unpopular but still worthwhile because it provided an essential forum for the minority who did agree with them. Hefley (1976) published a detailed description of the Gablers' strategies, such as the use of negative book reviews to persuade textbook adoption committees. In the cases of textbooks that had not been reviewed, the Gablers outlined procedures for making custom reviews that could document the presence of humanism, immorality, evolution, or the occult. They also adjured reviewers to search for textbook attacks upon religion, Christianity, or the Bible.

Kealey (1980) had reviewed the image of the family in second-grade reading materials. Like the Gablers, he adjured educators to confirm that textbooks reinforced Christian values centering about two-parent families. After tabulating references to families with two parents, he contrasted these with the references to alternatively organized families. He noted that while 17 percent of the children in the United States lived in single-parent families, 38 percent of the children depicted in basal readers came from single-parent families. Kealey warned teachers that such books undermined Christian values.

Kretman and Parker (1986) reported that a panel of educators and historians had determined that most recent United States history books were significantly better than the older ones. Despite this positive evaluation, the panel thought that the role of religion in the United States had been under-stated. Publishers recognized that their book would be marketed to a heterogeneous group comprising atheists and fundamentalists. Not surprisingly, these two reporters speculated that the omission of religious content might have been a calculated marketing decision.

Table 5.2   Criticism of Religious Bias in Textbooks during the Second Half of the Twentieth Century

[Some Muslims], to the surprise of the Christians present, complained that history textbooks used in the schools of Europe and America were not sympathetic to Islam." (Lauwerys, 1953)

At no time have American history textbooks for grades seven and eight been given a balanced presentation of religion in American history." (Howley, 1959)

Specialists in intergroup relations have long contended that world history texts could do much to counteract the 'Christ-killer' concept in anti-Semitism." (Marcus, 1961)

Our heritage, this nation's Christian heritage and the scriptural principles on which it was founded, are omitted and only a materialistic view given." (Remarks made in 1961 by Norma Gabler about an American history book, quoted by Hefley, 1976)

The evolutionary origin of the universe, of life and of man is taught as scientific fact [in textbooks while]…the Christian and Biblical record of origins is usually ignored, sometimes allegorized or even ridiculed." (Morris, 1963)

It is almost incredible that evolution has still to be bootlegged into some science texts as organic development." (Jennings, 1964)

[Social Studies Textbooks] have no reference to God or religion." (Price, 1966)

[An independent, nonprofit group of scientists and teachers funded by the federal government to develop biology books] replaced, 'Biologists are convinced that the human species evolved from nonhuman forms,' with a statement that 'Many biologists assume that the human species evolved from nonhuman forms.'" (Black, 1967)

[High school sociology textbooks] are teaching the young to hate family loyalty, Christian morality and Christian individuals." (Carle, 1972)

During public hearings in Texas for the statewide adoption of textbooks, critics charged a 5th-grade text I had written with…blasphemy in mentioning the ideas of Thoreau, Gandhi, and Martin Luther King Jr. in the same breadth with Jesus." (Remarks about a 1972 textbook hearing, Jacobs, 1983)

"The textbook battle is…a necessary effort of ordinary families determined to preserve and live their Christian way of life." (Conlan, 1976)

Continued on next page

Table 5.2   (Continued)

[Humanistic textbook authors] do not believe in God and, of course, they do not believe in salvation or damnation." (Conn, 1978)

[Anti-Christian humanists who wish to subvert Christianity are] controlling the textbooks that are used from the primary schools through the universities." (Duncan, 1979)

We are biased against those books...which challenge, mock or shatter cherished myths." (Rovenger, 1983)

It is the fault of a nation and its leaders who have abandoned our roots and seek to keep others from rediscovering them by censoring traditional [Christian] values from textbooks." (Thomas, 1983)

For the most part these [best selling social studies] books place religion at the lunatic fringe of American society." (Palsey, 1987)

From evangelical and pentecostal [*sic*] organizations come demands to [make textbooks] endorse creationism and an absolute set of traditional values." (Sewall, 1988)

Muslims complained that the textbooks' coverage of Islam mentions historical aggressiveness and religious passion aimed at the infidel and treats their religion as the gospel of ignorant nomads." (Kirp, 1991)

Vitz (1986) found that the only references to God or religion in elementary social studies books were in patriotic proclamations such as the Pledge of Allegiance. Although he observed occasional photographs of churches, Spanish missions, and Pilgrims, these usually were not accompanied by textual information. A year later, Palsey (1987) agreed that religious events and personalities were absent from history textbooks. When he did locate information about the Puritans, he was still displeased because they were depicted as "authoritarian crackpots." As examples of grave textbook omissions, he cited failures to acknowledge the role of religion in the abolition, temperance, and women's rights movements.

Table 5.2 (p. 123) contains quotations about religiously biased textbooks. The remarks, which were made during the second half of the twentieth century, reveal a failure to resolve the contentious issues from earlier eras.

Stereotyping Jews

Jews and Christians were not treated comparably in early twentieth-century textbooks. As an example, Thompson (1917) did not evenhandedly describe sectarian strife during the colonial period. Though he conceded that this "period was characterized by religious intolerance and persecution," he pointed out that Jews and Catholics "were particularly obnoxious to the great bulk of the population" (p. 36). He noted that even though "the colonists hated the Jews," they did allow them "to live in larger towns, and even to have their own places of worship." Later in the book, he compared the Jews to the Chinese and argued that both groups were incapable of being assimilated. However, he did not think Jews had been victims of discrimination because "their isolation is the result of their own choice, and caused by their religion" (p. 366).

Burnham (1920) wrote in his American history textbook about the plight of immigrants attempting to escape religious persecution. With regard to the Jews, he noted simply that "many Jews are in America because of the persecution of their race in Russia" (p. 546). However, this sentence was followed by the remark that "probably the hope of making a better living in the United States than they have ever known at home has lured the greatest number." Contrast this with his description of Puritan colonists:

> The colonists brought some of the finest thoughts and noblest ideals of the world. Many of them dared the stormy Atlantic because: "They sought a faith's pure shrine." The splendid literature of England, the highest standards of conduct and character of their time, and the purest Christian faith and life were the priceless possessions of many of our earliest American ancestors. (p. 68)

Aware that some students might be confused by his compliments about Puritan character in view of their cruel persecution of witches, Burnham rationalized that "in the European countries from which the colonists came witchcraft had long been punished by death, and it is not strange that the early American settlers should inflict the same penalty upon those they thought to be in league with the evil one" (p. 68). Although he conceded that 20 persons had been killed for witchcraft in 1692, he added that others who had been jailed were released, that the Puritans themselves were "sincerely repentant," and that "since the famous Salem delusion there has never been an execution for witchcraft in our country." Burnham made no reference to the repression of Jews during this era.

Five years earlier, Ashley (1915) had published an American history textbook in which he also attempted to explain the "delusions" by Christians in Salem. He reassured students that a belief in witchcraft, even though undeniable among the Puritans, was still "much less common in England than on the continent, and less common here than in England, although the non-English immigrants were very superstitious" (p. 116). He added that the executions would not have happened were it not for "afflicted children" who were "under the morbid training of some ignorant colored servants" (p. 117). The suppression of Jews' rights was referred to in a single sentence, when Ashley observed that eventually "the old demand that no one should vote unless he held certain religious views was discarded" and that consequently both Jews and Catholics acquired political rights that were formerly restricted to Protestants.

Another textbook author from this era, Fite (1919) discussed witchcraft and other colonial era persecutions. With regard to witchcraft, he concluded that the "Puritan extremes, terrible as they were, were generally to be ascribed to a passion for duty" (p. 56). He buttressed this explanation with the observation that "the intensity of repentance was as deep as the original excitement." Fite made no mention of Jewish persecution. However, he did elaborate about "distressed Romanists" for whom "refuge was sorely needed" (p. 57). He wrote approvingly of priests committed to "the spread of Christianity among the natives." He characterized the Jesuits "as a remarkable Roman Catholic order" and judged that "finer devotion to Christian ideals was never exhibited, greater dangers and sufferings in the name of religion never encountered" (p. 85).

Condon (1928) wrote a reading textbook in which the passages were selected with a conscious determination to avoid creating "a feeling of intolerance or controversy" about religious issues. Despite Condon's confident assurance that he had eschewed religious biases, he included a set of World War I letters written by "a Hebrew soldier" to his mother. These letters described how the young man was so inspired by Sunday "regimental Church services" that he "determined hereafter to attend them every Sunday" (p. 83).

By the 1930s, many American history textbooks were depicting the Ku Klux Klan as a criminal organization that had demonstrated prejudice and brutality toward African Americans. However, almost no textbooks mentioned the Klan's discrimination against Jews. Hamm's textbook (1938) stood out from others, even though it contained a single sentence acknowledging that the Klan's "ill will and discrimination" was aimed at Jews and Catholics as well as African Americans.

Davis-Dubois (1935) traced the source of anti-Jewish prejudice to three causes: the classroom use of the *Merchant of Venice*, theories about a superior race, and the conviction that all Jews were responsible for the death of Christ. Although two of these factors were largely noneducational, Davis-Dubois was convinced that they had been nurtured by educators who had failed to combat anti-Semitism. Almost fifteen years later, the American Council on Education (1949) expressed the opposite view. The committee's members thought that educators should not feel guilty when their students referred to Jews with negative epithets because these terms had been learned outside school. Although they noted instances of textbook bias, they concluded that these were too infrequent to cause any social tension. Despite the nonculpability of teachers and textbooks, instructors were counseled to clarify the circumstances of Jesus' death in ways that would dispel any anti-Jewish prejudices.

In the early 1950s, Roy (1953) disagreed with the American Council on Education's sanguine assessment about the absence of religious discord in the schools. In the initial sentence of a book with the inflammatory title *Apostles of Discord*, he warned that Protestantism was being threatened by "organized malcontents who zealously seek to promote hate and disruption under the banner of the Christian faith" (p. ix). Among the scores of incidents he reviewed were activities by the Textbook Commission to Eliminate Anti-Semitic Statements in American Textbooks. Roy accused this artfully named group of actually increasing hostility to Jews. He buttressed this allegation with critical remarks about the textbook commission from the American Jewish Committee and the Anti-Defamation League of B'nai B'rith.

Writing during the same period, Stewart (1950) reported the conclusions of an investigation by a committee of the National Conference of Christians and Jews.

> The committee found that the textbooks and courses of study were, with very few exceptions, free of intentional bias toward any group in the American population. It found, however, many instances of careless wording which tended to perpetuate antagonisms now current in American life. Many examples of inaccurate writing, revealing a hidden bias, might be given. One text, for instance, links Jews and atheists in a sequence of groups. Another ties "Jews and Communists." (p. 5)

Stewart also noted that most of the material about Jews in textbooks concerned ancient Judaism. As a consequence, students might be left with the impression that these ancient beliefs were identical with those maintained by current Jewish communities or that Judaism had ceased to be a vibrant force in the modern world.

Like Stewart, Harris (1963) reviewed the treatment of Jews in textbooks. Similar to the observations made by Stewart 13 years earlier, she noted that in those textbooks that dealt with Jewish history, "a typical text begins with the journey of Abraham and his followers, recounts the Egyptian persecution, the Exodus and conquest of Israel, David and Solomon, the division of the kingdom, and the eventual dispersion" (p. 28). She reported that only a single elementary-school social studies textbook had referred to the activities of Jews during any aspect of the eighteenth century. Of 11 textbooks, only five mentioned the suppression of Jews during Hitler's regime, and one of these took a neutral stance. Less than a decade later, Kane (1970) examined the treatment of Jews in social studies books and concluded that negative portrayals had been eliminated. However, he was still disturbed that the former stereotypes had not been replaced by positive portrayals.

Summary

Although early nineteenth-century textbooks were heavily Christian, publishers reduced this content when the central position of religion in society shifted. Irate critics promoted classroom Bible reading as an antidote. However, they insisted on blacklisting textbooks with information about evolution or secular philosophies. The banning of information about evolution was nationally publicized during the 1920s prosecution of a high-school teacher in Tennessee. Additional allegations about irreligious textbooks continued throughout the century.

CHAPTER SIX

Textbooks as Learning Tools— The Pedagogical Era

Publishers refined textbooks by manipulating physical materials, vocabulary, grammar, organization, design, and pedagogy. Though they acknowledged that textbooks were becoming more efficient, critics warned that the improved materials were suppressing teacher creativity. Critics also predicted that an emerging technology would replace textbooks. Despite censure and negative predictions, textbooks dominated classroom learning throughout the century.

Textbook Legibility

Educators and publishers first attempted to improve textbooks by concentrating on their physical features. In a late nineteenth-century study about the effects of different sizes of print, Sanford (1888) wrote that he was searching for "any device of paper or ink or type" to facilitate reading. Several years later, Griffing and Franz (1896) referred to the work of Sanford when they divided reading problems into two categories, readers and books. The book problems included size of print, color of paper, length of lines, and spacing. Edmund Huey (1900) gave explicit advice about a book's type, which he thought should be selected to promote efficient eye movements rather than to save paper and ink.

The fourth edition of an English textbook by Reed and Kellogg (1905) revealed the impact of such research reports. In remarks attached to the cover and addressed to textbook reviewers, the publishers acknowledged that "few changes were needed to bring the book into complete harmony with the views of the highest authorities." Even though they had made no significant changes, the publishers stressed that "advantage has been taken of the necessity for making new electrotype plates to set the book in larger and more beautiful type." In a 1906 advertisement for the Longmans' series of English books, the publisher included a quote in which one reviewer noted approvingly that "the binding and typography are ideal" and that "the American school-boy is to be congratulated that he at length may study his English from books in so attractive a dress" (Passage from an advertisement that appeared on the final page of a textbook by Bates, 1906).

Writing in a typography journal, Koopman (1909b) reviewed 25 years of research about print's relationship to eye movements. This research persuaded him that the most legible print was simple, uniform, wide, heavy, and large. In another report published that same year, Koopman (1909a) urged educators and printers to work together to design textbooks with the best possible print. Burnham, Small, and Standish (1911) delineated standards for schoolbook type, paper, and margins. The features for the type to be used with first grade materials demonstrated the specificity of these standards:

(i) The heights of the small letters should be at lest 2.6mm., with the other dimensions in proportion.
(ii) The width of the vertical stroke should be from .4mm. to .5 mm.
(iii) The space within the letters should be from .8mm. to .9 mm.
(iv) The space between the letters should be about 1 mm.
(v) The space between the words should be about 3 mm.
(vi) The leading should be from 4 mm. to 4.5 mm. (p. 255)

These authors also recommended paper that was unglazed, dull, opaque, and sufficiently lightweight that students could carry the textbooks made from it without a struggle. The authors added that they had not yet decided on the optimal color for textbook paper, but they thought it might be either white or some slightly tinted variation.

The fascination with legibility was evident even in the design of school furniture. Figure 6.1 is a World War I era advertisement for a desk with a surface that tilted to reduce textbook glare and present print at the optimal reading angle.

Readability

By the 1920s, publishers and educators had realized that the mere alteration of paper, print, and spacing would not sufficiently improve textbooks (Gilliland, 1923). As a consequence, educational researchers began to look at different factors. This shift had been anticipated by William McGuffey, who had created his extremely popular nineteenth-century reading textbooks with attention to the "gradation" of content. In an 1879 preface to his *First Eclectic Reader*, McGuffey had written that "words of only two or three letters are used in the first lessons" and that "longer and more difficult ones are gradually introduced" (1920, p. iii). At the end of a textbook by Emerson and Bender (1915), the publisher included advertisements for other textbooks. Grading was judged to be such a critical marketing feature for one of these series that

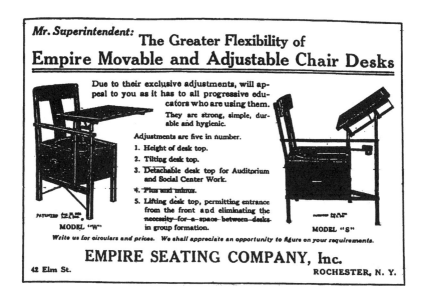

Figure 6.1 World War I Era Desks with Tops that Tilted
to Promote Efficient Textbook Reading

it was named the *Graded City Spellers*. However, no reference was made to the system by which the spellers were graded. With regard to a promotion of a set of literature books by Baker, Carpenter, and Robbins, the publisher acknowledged that much had been "sacrificed" in order to assure that the initial volumes in this series were appropriately graded. In this case, the grading had been done by the editors with "the assistance of able and experienced teachers."

McGuffey's early intuition that vocabulary was a key determinant of effective textbooks eventually became accepted by most textbook publishers. However, numerous other factors seemed equally plausible to educational researchers. Judd (1918) endorsed a 6-item checklist with which to systematically distinguish effective reading materials. Agreeing with Judd that textbooks needed to be selected in a systematic manner, Otis (1923) reviewed Judd's checklist as well as several others, but criticized them because each could be used exclusively with materials from a single academic area. He then developed a "score card" that was suited to a broad range of textbooks. His score card highlighted organization, instructional aids, mechanical features, and subject matter. Other score cards from this era (Horn, 1922; Fowlkes, 1923; Donovan, 1924) used evaluative criteria that included ability to stimulate interest, likelihood of comprehension, study aids, organization, illustrations, mechanical construction, enduring value of the content, method of study, expertise of the authors, and adaptability for multiple learning environments.

On a four-category checklist for high-school textbooks, Johnson (1925) included general information, subject matter, physical features, and aids to instruction. He provided extremely specific questions under each category to assist teachers and administrators. As an example of this specificity, he listed 12 questions under "aids to instruction" and directed evaluators to examine a textbook's preface, introduction, table of contents, index, glossary, appendix, illustrations, references, summaries, study guides, review questions, and drilling exercises.

Summarizing factors for assessing textbooks, Patty and Painter (1931) listed several features that had emerged during the 1920s. Although they did call attention to vocabulary, it was only one of many items. This initial reluctance to emphasize vocabulary diminished as researchers began to search for mathematically formatted formulas with which to classify books as "readable" or "non-readable." Thorndike (1921) computed the frequency with which 10,000 words occurred and used this as the basis for an early formula to assess the difficulty of reading materials. Two years later, Lively and Pressey (1923) described a more elaborate procedure in which teachers extracted 1000-word passages from a book and then used Thorndike's list to determine the frequency of those words. Vogel and Washburne (1928) developed a still more complex formula that relied upon a passage's number of prepositions, the heterogeneity of the vocabulary, the number of simple sentences, and the frequency of occurrence for any words in the passage that were not included on Thorndike's list.

Because readability formulas were impractical and confusing, publishers were reluctant to employ them. In the advertisement for a popular American history textbook (Freeland, Walker, & Williams, 1937), the publisher adjured teachers that "as you examine this book please keep in mind four main points," one of which was that the book was "outstandingly easy to read." Instead of identifying the readability formula that had been used to confirm this feature, the publisher simply indicated that "the vocabulary has been most carefully checked with standard word lists and the sentence structure expertly simplified with no loss in content or pleasing effect."

Though publishers thought that the readability formulas were impractical, researchers did not initially change them. Johnson (1930) was one of the first educators to recommend a simpler readability procedure in which teachers calculated the frequency with which polysyllabic words occurred. However, it would be several decades before this type of uncomplicated approach would

Figure 6.2 Advertisement for a 1930s Textbook that Indicated a Reluctance to Identify a Readability Formula

become popular. Late into the 1960s, Fang (1967) was still able to observe that "the trouble with most readability formulas is that they are as long-winded and difficult to understand as the worst sentences they measure" (p. 63). Just a year later though, Fry (1968) proposed a readability measure that was explained on two pages of text and that could be calculated in only several minutes. Fry's brief formula was used so extensively that less than a decade later Singer (1975) concluded that all of the popular readability formulas exhibited comparable simplicity.

Pictorial Aids

During the nineteenth century, charts, tables, maps, graphs, and documents were not included in most textbooks. Instead, they were sold in large tablets that teachers placed on tripods for use with their entire class. Figure 6.2 (p. 133) is a late nineteenth-century advertisement for some of these economical textbook supplements.

Teachers also had the option of purchasing special supplementary readers that could enrich barren textbooks. Figure 6.3 (p. 135) is an advertisement for early twentieth-century geographical readers that were "well supplied with colored maps and illustrations" and that were designed to be used "in connection with the regular textbooks on geography or history."

At the very end of the nineteenth century, publishers began to market books that incorporated instructional aids such as those highlighted in Figures 6.2 (p. 133) and 6.3 (p. 135). This trend was especially apparent in social studies materials. Mowry and Mowry (1897) wrote an American history textbook and noted on the title page that the book was filled "with maps, illustrations, analyses, and bibliographies." A decade earlier, Higbee (1888) boasted that no country was producing textbooks that surpassed those made in the United States. He added that this quality was apparent not only in the books' content but also in their physical workmanship and appearance. He lamented that so many persons took textbooks for granted that first-rate materials were scattered in the schools as "thick as autumnal leaves."

During the twentieth century, textbook illustrations were handled with the same attention that earlier had been reserved for format and physical construction. Ginn (1910) reported that publishing firms were spending a "great deal" on textbook pictures. He noted that the average cost for illustrating a textbook had risen to several hundred dollars, but that certain types of books, such as those in geography, might require $20,000 to $30,000. Figure 6.4 (p. 136) contains illustrations from an early twentieth-century geography textbook (Trotter 1906). Though these illustrations seemed humble even a decade later, they were lavish compared to those in the other types of contemporary textbooks.

Carpenter's Geographical Readers

By FRANK G. CARPENTER

North America. Cloth, 12mo, 352 pages .   . 60 cents

South America. Cloth, 12mo, 352 pages .   . 60 cents

Asia. Cloth, 12mo, 304 pages .   .   .   . 60 cents

These new Geographical Readers are by far the most attractive and instructive books of their kind ever published. They are not mere compilations of other books or stories of imaginary travels, but they are the results of the author's actual journeys through the different countries, with personal observations of their native peoples, just as they are found to-day in their homes and at their work. These journeys and visits are described in such simple and engaging manner as to make the books as entertaining as stories, while conveying in this attractive way, useful knowledge and information. While they are written in easy familiar style, and in language not above the comprehension of children, they are strictly accurate in every detail and statement.

The books are well supplied with colored maps and illustrations, the latter mostly reproductions from original photographs taken by the author on the ground. They combine studies in geography with stories of travel and observation in a manner at once attractive and instructive. Their use in connection with the regular text-books on geography and history will impart a fresh and living interest to their lessons.

Copies of Carpenter's Geographical Readers will be sent, prepaid, to any address on receipt of the price by the Publishers :

American Book Company

New York   •   Cincinnati   •   Chicago

(15)

Figure 6.3 Early Twentieth-Century Advertisement for Special Materials to Supplement Textbooks with Limited Illustrations

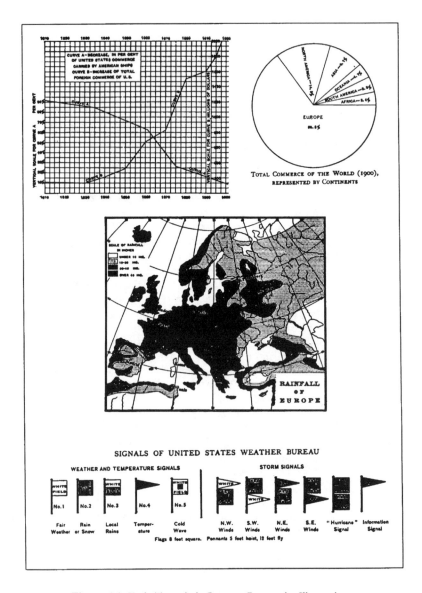

Figure 6.4 Early Twentieth-Century Geography Illustrations
Were Considered Lavish

In a 1907 advertisement for a different geography book, the publishers
noted that there were 568 photographs, with which "no other text-book can

compare." The publisher added parenthetically that the photographs were so well done that they provided the best experiences, "next to being on the ground" (Passage from an advertisement at the rear of a textbook, Tarr & McMurry, 1907). In a 1907 promotion for an astronomy book, the publisher bragged that "the illustrations demand special mention" because "many of them are so ingeniously devised that they explain at a glance what many pages of description could not make clear (Passage from an advertisement on the final page of a textbook, Hunter, 1907).

Stillwell (1919) wrote about the tremendous expertise and effort needed to create textbook illustrations.

> The author furnishes the copy, either photographs or drawings, or requests the publisher to provide them at the author's expense. The drawings may be reproduced as line engravings or half-tones. Black and white or line drawings are reproduced on zinc, briefly in the following manner: The drawing is photographed the desired size and printed on a sensitized zinc plate. The background is then etched out by acid leaving the drawing in relief. Washing drawings and photographs are photographed on copper. This is called a half-tone. Zinc plates print well on book paper (unsized), so they are more commonly found in schoolbooks than half-tones, which demand a highly finished paper. Colored pictures may be printed from either zinc plates or half-tones, but a separate plate must be made for each color. Different shades and tints, however, are produced not by separate plates but by printing one color over another. (pp. 261–262)

Writing a year earlier, Mead (1918) advised teachers to select textbooks with photographs, diagrams, tables, or graphs. Thomas (1924) reported that publishers were consulting extensively with artists, engravers, printers, and bookbinders in order to create "a faultless piece of work." Agreeing that the publisher's goal was to develop "a thing of beauty" as well as a functional learning aid, Donovan (1924) concluded that the best textbooks were "so well bound, so beautifully decorated, and so perfectly printed on the best paper that it appears doubtful that notable further improvement along these lines will be achieved" (p. 1).

The number of pictures included in textbooks increased dramatically during the early twentieth century. As one indication of this trend, the members of the Association for Peace Education (1923) analyzed the illustrations in the history textbooks published between 1904 and 1922. Although they noted that the number of illustrations about war had risen noticeably, the authors attributed this to the greater number of illustrations in newer books. Knowlton (1925) wrote that effective textbooks should "abound" with pictures, maps, and diagrams. He added that "if a picture will tell the story better, or if it will add details of real value to the child as he tries to call up the scene, it is as important an asset to the teacher as is the text itself." Writing during this same period, Maxwell (1921) also noted the increasing numbers of textbook pictures as well as their concomitant expense. After remarking that the illustrations in some recent textbooks had cost more than the manuscripts, he warned of a backlash against pictorial extravagances. Nonetheless, he was confident that publishers would never return "to the dry, formal, unattractive textbooks that tended to make children feel that school was the place where anything beautiful was not to be tolerated." Chase and Cornforth (1932) counted the illustrations related to World War I in 11 popular junior high history textbooks. The number of illustrations about just this single topic ranged from a single volume low of three to a book with 28. These researchers asked educators to decide if some authors were ignoring valuable resources by restricting the use of pictures or whether others were profligately taking space that could have been devoted more wisely to text.

Rugg (1930) wrote in the preface to a popular social studies textbook that he had employed "a wealth of maps, graphs, and pictorial materials far in excess of their present use in textbooks" (p. vii). Rugg's book was over six hundred pages long and contained several hundred illustrations. Among the innovative illustrations that Rugg selected were reproductions of newspaper headlines and stories. However, Rugg's pictorial portfolio seemed inadequate just ten years later. By the 1940s, the number of illustrations in social studies textbooks had tripled and in some cases quadrupled. As one example, a geography textbook by Jones and Darkenwald (1941) contained 390 photographs and 400 maps or charts. To ensure that school personnel would be aware of these illustrations, they cited each one in lists displayed prominently at the beginning of their book. Needless to say, some of the illustrations packed into these types of textbooks had questionable learning value.

Not just illustrations but color pictures became common. In a 1916 advertisement for a popular set of reading materials by Baker, Carpenter, and Robbins (1906), the publisher noted that color illustrations created by "new processes" had been included to provide "special charm." In his advice for evaluating textbooks, Andrews (1926) directed teachers to assure that color illustrations were included and also to confirm that they were attached securely and not just pasted in as an afterthought. A 1920s American history textbook (Gordy, 1925) noted on the title page that it was "illustrated in black and white and color." Another book published that same year was even more explicit, noting on the title page that it was "illustrated with three hundred and thirty-four engravings in black and white, fifty-one maps, and eight color plates from the J. L. G. Ferris collection of American historical paintings" (Burnham, 1920). Brammer (1967) observed that an immensely successful 1930s reading series with full-color pictures had prodded competing publishers into using comparably expensive illustrations. Full-color textbook illustrations had become standard by the end of the 1940s. Although they were initially pleased with the marketing advantages that the color illustrations created, publishers complained later about their expense.

Knowlton (1950) disdainfully observed that though the colored illustrations were beautiful, they often lacked educational value. For several decades, other critics continued to make this point. More than 35 years later, Marquand (1985b) was still warning of the questionable marketing strategies that textbook publishers were employing to highlight the illustrations in their materials. As an example, they were placing the largest and most colorful illustrations on the right sides of pages only so that busy reviewers who were thumbing through texts would have a higher likelihood of noticing them. Woodward (1989) agreed that marketing rather than pedagogy was responsible for the increased number of textbook illustrations. He described the illustrations in most textbooks as mere collages of pretty pictures that sometimes preempted 50 percent of the available space. The value of portraits, ceremonial photos, and uncaptioned pictures seemed especially questionable.

Though some educators challenged both the pedagogical benefits of illustrations and the motivation of publishers for including them in textbooks, and though many publishers were wary of the increased expenses, most persons were confident that lavish illustrations helped students. Edgerton (1969) judged that even costly pictures were wise investments because they used the least amount of space to effectively convey concepts. Convinced that those who were not currently learning from textbook illustrations still could, he advised teachers to actively train students to rely on pictures.

O'Brien (1988), a secondary teacher who had written the teachers' resource manual for a popular social studies textbook, judged that most teachers were drawn to textbooks because of illustrations that made abstract concepts accessible or photographs that glamorized uninteresting subjects. A year earlier, a publication of the American Federation of Teachers (1987) had made a somewhat similar concession when it noted that the authority of textbooks increased if they had expensive appearances and numerous color illustrations.

Influence of Textbooks on Teachers

In a book subtitled *Teaching without Textbooks,* Beechold (1971) wrote cynically that instructors who used textbooks became classroom agents for publishers.

He ticked off reasons why teachers should reject textbooks, warning that they "tie down both teacher and student through de facto control of the curriculum," "enmesh the teacher in a tangle of 'guides,'" are "written down to the lowest common denominator," are "tastelessly designed," and are "filled with outright misinformation." He added that they were "the antithesis of creativity," "monumentally boring," and "tiresome things to bother with" (p. 283).

Decades before Beechold had fired this broadside, critics and advocates of textbooks had tried to resolve whether textbooks had a deleterious influence on teachers. Miller (1916) represented those extreme, progressive educators who, like Beechold, had judged textbooks to be completely dispensable. Miller developed a curriculum in American history that was intended for primary and rural schools and that was to be taught exclusively through stories, songs, and activities. Though Miller included key historical information in her book, this material was to be read solely by the teacher and then communicated orally to the students.

Although progressive educators belittled them, textbook advocates considered their materials beneficial and even indispensable. They particularly resented the characterization of textbook publishers as crass opportunists intent on making profits at children's expense. For example, Ginn (1910) pointed out that his publishing firm employees were professionals who were committed to helping teachers. He depicted even the sales agents as carefully recruited specialists who distributed free instructional materials, listened sensitively to educators, and conveyed their concerns to editors. Fitzpatrick (1912) agreed that book agents were professionals who were just as concerned about improving instruction as selling materials.

Textbook advocates also disagreed with the depiction of their materials as molds into which mindless teachers forced malleable learners. In their reading book, Arnold and Gilbert (1898) included a special section about how teachers should design effective textbook lessons. They stressed that teaching "should by no means be confined to the use of school readers" and that students should often consult other textbooks and library materials. They advised teachers to confirm that lessons were successful by asking students to relate the textbook material to "the other subjects of their school course, to literature, and to life" (p. xi). In the case of another set of reading materials, William McGuffey had called his popular textbooks "eclectic readers" precisely because they encouraged teacher creativity. The revised edition of these readers (McGuffey, 1920) still contained the original 1879 section with "suggestions to teachers." This section described popular approaches to reading education and assured teachers that the textbook could "be used in teaching reading by any of the methods in common use" or in fact by combinations of these approaches. The editor of a popular literature anthology (Bates 1906) that had been published originally in 1861 advised teachers to allow the students themselves to select the poems for memorization because these "would be learned with more enthusiasm" (p. xiv). Bates also discouraged assignments in which students would write formal reports about authors or their works because these would likely be "condensed from—if not copied from—the handiest book of reference." In a reading textbook published that same year, Baker, Carpenter, and Robbins (1906) wrote that they wished to make student interest the hallmark of their readers. Although this goal had been compromised by the need to employ simple language in the first two volumes, each of the subsequent volumes had distinctive, stimulating themes such as fairy stories, folktales, animal stories, tales of adventure, and great myths of the world.

When they were characterizing textbooks as deterrents to creativity, critics focused in a special way on the grammar books, which they judged to be the archetypes of regimentation. In the preface to a popular early twentieth-century grammar book, Kimball (1900) positioned herself as a target by stating that it was "universally conceded" that the primary purpose for studying grammar was to "discipline the mind." However, other authors disagreed with her strict pedagogical philosophy. For example, Prince (1910) wrote an early twentieth-century grammar book in which he argued that his materials were not to be used unilaterally with all students. He disapproved of textbooks that required "an endless mass of facts" not "of any immediate use to the pupils" (p. iii). Although his book provided instructional guidance and support, he indicated that it was intended "only as a hint to the teacher of what should be done to prepare pupils for the study of grammar." In the preface to an English textbook published originally in 1909, Emerson and Bender (1915) wrote that their book recognized "the supreme importance of interest in successful language study" (p. v). They emphasized "the cultivation of the imagination" through oral language activities that built on the child's school as well as home knowledge. Figure 6.5 (p. 142) contains one of their exercises illustrating this assumption.

In an English book published originally in 1921, Law (1927) wrote a preface for teachers in which he acknowledged that his text was focused chiefly on "writing for practical purposes." He included chapters corresponding to realistic situations such as telling jokes, making requests, retelling the news, writing stories for school newspapers, providing opinions, and advertising. Crumpton's (1928) views of the adaptable, incidental, and informal nature of her English textbook were evident when she noted in the

—— 157 ——

A LOST CHILD

An Exercise in Story Making

Little May, aged three — follows brother — lost!
Strange streets and sights — kind people — questions — "Mother's name?"   "Mamma!" — ribbon with card, address — safe at home.

Figure 6.5 A 1915 English Textbook Activity Designed
to Elicit Creative Oral Language

preface that "each unit of this book is introduced by questions, games, exercises, or projects" that were "drawn from the life and interests of the pupils themselves" (p. iii). Each activity was to be performed "naturally" so that the learner was "intent only on the pleasure he can receive from it." Smith, Magee, and Seward (1928) wrote in the teacher's preface that their grammar book contained sections with abridged materials and illustrations that would be especially useful to the "slow and the backward student." Jones (1935) included special reviews intended for "remedial work with students differing widely in preparation" (p. v.). Tressler and Shelmadine (1940) opened the preface with the statement that their book was based on a philosophy in which "every pupil-experience or situation in and out of school that stimulates self-expression offers an opportunity for developing language ability."

Winship (1915) had insisted that effective learning assumed textbooks as well as teachers. In an earlier report, his salutary view of textbooks was even more obvious when he wrote that "even a poor teacher cannot prevent a child's learning a subject if he has a good book" (Winship, 1908, p. 339). In

Tarr and McMurry's Geographies

A New Series of Geographies in Two, Three, or Five Volumes

By RALPH S. TARR, B.S., F.G.S.A.
CORNELL UNIVERSITY
AND
FRANK M. McMURRY, Ph.D.
TEACHERS COLLEGE, COLUMBIA UNIVERSITY

TWO BOOK SERIES

Introductory Geography	60 cents
Complete Geography	$1.00

THE THREE BOOK SERIES

FIRST BOOK (4th and 5th years) Home Geography and the Earth as a Whole	60 cents
SECOND BOOK (6th year) North America	75 cents
THIRD BOOK (7th year) Europe and Other Continents	75 cents

THE FIVE BOOK SERIES

FIRST PART (4th year) Home Geography	40 cents
SECOND PART (5th year) The Earth as a Whole	40 cents
THIRD PART (6th year) North America	75 cents
FOURTH PART (7th year) Europe, South America, etc.	50 cents
FIFTH PART (8th year) Asia and Africa, with Review of North America (with State Supplement)	50 cents
Without Supplement	40 cents
Home Geography, Greater New York Edition	50 cents
Teachers' Manual of Method in Geography. By CHARLES A. McMURRY	40 cents

To meet the requirements of some courses of study, the section from the Third Book, treating of South America, is bound up with the Second Book, thus bringing North America and South America together in one volume.

The following Supplementary Volumes have also been prepared, and may be had separately or bound together with the Third Book of the Three Book Series, or the Fifth Part of the Five Book Series:

SUPPLEMENTARY VOLUMES

New York State	30 cents	Kansas	30 cents
The New England States	30 cents	Virginia	30 cents
Utah	40 cents	Pennsylvania	30 cents
California	30 cents	Tennessee	30 cents
Ohio	30 cents	Louisiana	30 cents
Illinois	30 cents	Texas	35 cents
New Jersey	30 cents		

When ordering, be careful to specify the Book or Part and the Series desired, and whether with or without the State Supplement.

THE MACMILLAN COMPANY
64-66 FIFTH AVENUE, NEW YORK
BOSTON   CHICAGO   ATLANTA   SAN FRANCISCO

Figure 6.6 A 1916 Advertisement that Appealed to
Teachers' Discretion to Select Books

response to those who contended that abandoning textbooks would enhance teacher creativity, Winship retorted that creativity would be advanced only among veteran instructors who restricted themselves to teaching solely in those subject areas in which they were experts. Although he conceded that anyone could use "brainless" books, he pointed out that the best textbooks nurtured teachers' instructional ingenuity.

Features of textbooks that nurtured teacher creativity and independence were highlighted in advertisements. Figure 6.6 (p. 143) contains a 1916 promotion for a series of geography books. Although the same two authors wrote all of the books that were listed, teachers could use their discretion about whether to adopt a two, three, or five book series. Additionally, the authors provided supplementary volumes on the geography of individual states that teachers could select and use.

Maxwell (1921) listed explicit benefits of textbooks. These positive features included maps, charts, tables, photographs, engravings, motivational exercises, review questions, critical problems, bibliographies of supplementary reading materials, organizational outlines at the beginnings of units, lists of key terms, and instructors' manuals. Figure 6.7 illustrates a single page from an early twentieth-century American history textbook (Ashley, 1915) into which the publisher incorporated several helpful features, including an illustration, a list of key figures, subheadings, and marginal notations.

Maxwell (1921) argued that textbooks had benefits that extended beyond special editorial features such as those illustrated in Figure 6.7. For example, by their very nature, textbooks organized key data that students needed to learn. They also incorporated the intellectual perspectives of experts in the field. Even supplementary learning activities and the pedagogical aids that were within them were of unusual value because they were based on the most current educational thought. He counseled both traditional and progressive educators to use their classroom time wisely by taking advantage of the skillfully organized content in textbooks. In the case of progressive educators, he thought textbooks could be special opportunities to supplement, reinforce, and extend the firsthand student experiences on which they placed such a high premium.

Another advocate of textbooks, Peck (1923) noted that publishers were recruiting teams of "super-teachers" to advise them on the best classroom strategies. Alluding to textbook authors who were experts on current pedagogy, publishers portrayed themselves as professionals who were raising scholastic standards (Thomas, 1924). Douglas (1924) wrote that teachers should resist the temptation to behave like those unskilled workers who blamed their professional failures on inadequate tools. He adjured teachers to admit that their failures resulted more frequently from ignorance about how to use textbooks than from the textbooks themselves.

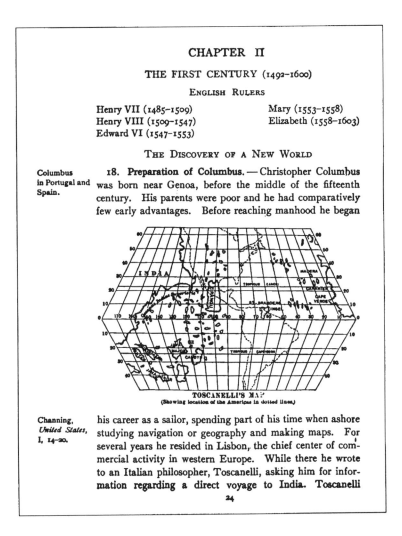

CHAPTER II

THE FIRST CENTURY (1492–1600)

ENGLISH RULERS

Henry VII (1485–1509)   Mary (1553–1558)
Henry VIII (1509–1547)   Elizabeth (1558–1603)
Edward VI (1547–1553)

THE DISCOVERY OF A NEW WORLD

Columbus in Portugal and Spain.

18. Preparation of Columbus. — Christopher Columbus was born near Genoa, before the middle of the fifteenth century. His parents were poor and he had comparatively few early advantages. Before reaching manhood he began

TOSCANELLI'S MAP
(Showing location of the Americas in dotted lines.)

Channing, *United States*, I, 14–20.

his career as a sailor, spending part of his time when ashore studying navigation or geography and making maps. For several years he resided in Lisbon, the chief center of commercial activity in western Europe. While there he wrote to an Italian philosopher, Toscanelli, asking him for information regarding a direct voyage to India. Toscanelli

24

Figure 6.7 Page from an Early Twentieth-Century Textbook Illustrating the Use of Graphics, Subtitles, Organizational Information, and Marginal Notes

In the teachers' manual for an American history textbook, Fish (1927) demonstrated a creative approach to textbook use by listing not only supplementary readings but personalized projects for each chapter. In the

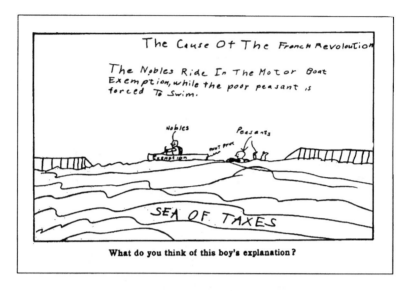

The Cause Of The French Revolution

The Nobles Ride In The Motor Boat Exemption, while the poor peasant is forced To Swim.

Nobles

Peasants

Exemption

SEA OF TAXES

What do you think of this boy's explanation?

Figure 6.8 Student-Created Art from a 1930s Textbook
Intended to Engender Critical Thinking

chapter on immigration, one of the projects was to "have students bring to class newspaper clippings to illustrate any of the topics discussed, such as means of crossing the Atlantic today; steamship advertisements, or articles on the Lakes-to-Ocean water route, or the development of the Mississippi" (p. 3). Edmonson and Dondineau (1927) wrote a civics textbook in which they also relied extensively on student problems. The title of their book, *Citizenship Through Problems*, highlighted this feature. They also noted that questions had been embedded within captions "to lead the pupils to find the real meaning of the illustrations" (p. viii). They were careful that "the book has been organized so that it may be readily adapted to one or to a variety of methods and hence maintain the individuality of the teacher" (p. ix). They gave examples of "newer methods of instruction" that their book complemented, specifically listing "the socialized recitation, individualized instruction, pupil participation, the project, the Dalton plan, and laboratory work."

Moore (1936) characterized his textbook as "dynamic throughout." This dynamism was apparent when he assured that the problems at the end of each chapter were there only for the "convenience of pupils and teachers." As such they "may be used or others substituted for them" or "some may be selected and others rejected" (p. vii). Another end-of-chapter feature, topics for reports, could be "used as stated or adapted to meet individual or special needs." Even with regard to the summary statement at the beginning of each chapter, he expected students to "debate it, accept it, or question it."

Parker, Patterson, and McAlister (1939) wrote a civics textbook for which they suggested instructional strategies that included extensive use of personal references, local environments, contemporary problems, and other books. A year earlier, Knowlton and Harden (1938) had also encouraged activities to help students personalize and think critically about their history textbook. Like many other authors, they included political cartoons to engender these skills. However, Knowlton and Harden also relied upon cartoons, maps, and drawings that had been made by students. These student-created projects illustrated how the learners using the textbook might approach their own projects. Additionally, the authors hoped that student-created pictures might engross learners and encourage them to think critically. Figure 6.8 is an example of one of these pictures.

Table 6.1 (p. 148) contains quotations about the pedagogical value of textbooks. These early twentieth-century remarks reveal the dichotomous perspectives from which the pedagogy of textbooks had been examined.

Lauwerys (1953) advised teachers to adapt textbooks by selecting suitable instructional approaches and supplementary materials. In an advertisement that was distributed with their American history textbook, Todd and Curti (1961) pointed out that each chapter concluded with sections designed to help instructors teach critical thinking, orchestrate group learning, and use materials to supplement their textbooks. Within the chapters themselves were "excerpts from selected American 'documents,' ranging from memorable speeches to significant characters." Furthermore, Todd and Curti supplemented their book with "the most comprehensive teaching aids program ever prepared." It included a teachers' resource guide, a student workbook, documents from American history, and phonograph records.

Price (1966) reported that some critics had been dismissing elementary social studies textbooks because of their superficial treatment of issues. Though he was an advocate for textbooks, Price responded bluntly that these charges were entirely true. He explained that textbooks incorporated only a portion of a curriculum's content and that individual teachers needed to provide supplementary materials and instruction. During the 1970s, the president of a large publishing house restated a popular defense of textbooks when he insisted that they did not homogenize classroom learning but rather saved classroom time that teachers then used to individualize learning (William Jovanovich, reported by Broudy, 1975).

**Table 6.1   Criticism of Textbook Pedagogy during the
First Half of the Twentieth Century**

"Recent [textbook] writers show many intimations of approaching perfection."
(Standing Committee on Textbooks, 1898)

"[I expect that teachers who adopt my textbook] will modify or extend topics and
references at will." (Passage from the preface for a history textbook, West, 1902)

"Better text-books can be made than are in use to-day." (Sabin, 1908)

"The deluge of text books…floods the educational world every year." (Stuart, 1910)

"The chief work of the pupil in school is the mastery of the text-books." (Harris,
1914)

"In the minds of many observers, both teachers and pupils in our schools are
suffering from too many text-books." ("School Text-books," 1915)

"Teachers and textbooks are analogous to men and tools of an industrial plant."
(Doughton, 1917)

"[The textbook] is put into the hands of teachers who are for the most part so limited
in experience and training that they never think of questioning the method suggested
by the book." (Judd, 1918)

"If the textbook does not lead, there is no guidance." (Butcher, 1919)

"[The textbook] has been used practically as a substitute for the teacher." (Cast,
1919)

"The textbook has become such a dominant force in the life of the American teacher
that it tends to determine the aims, the subject matter, and the method of instruction." (Woody, 1920)

"By the time the pupil has reached the junior high school he has become a textbook
addict." (Knowlton, 1925)

"Probably the most important of the forces directly responsible for American
education has been the creation of the high standard American textbook." (Cubberly,
1926)

Continued on next page

Table 6.1 (Continued)

"It is impossible to ascertain to what extent the intellectual power of children has been destroyed by the wrong use of textbooks." (Bode, 1928)

"It is probable that in many cases the textbook has had more influence in shaping the curriculum than the teacher has had." (Tidwell, 1928)

"I can imagine educators who might regard the discussion of the textbook as a waste of time on the grounds that the textbook is destined soon to pass out of use." (Whipple, 1930)

"[A textbook's] decisive influence is ever a factor to be reckoned with." (Compton, 1932)

"The traditional slavish use of a textbook for purposes of daily assignments and oral recitation has merited the criticisms that have been heaped upon it by progressive teachers." (Stormzand & Lewis, 1935)

"Texts could not retain their favor, if they had not to some degree met the criticisms to which they have been subjected." (Wilder, 1937)

Table 6.2 (p. 150) contains later twentieth-century quotations about the pedagogical value of textbooks. Not substantively different from the remarks made during the early part of the century, the quotes indicate the sustained, extensive use of textbooks as well as continuing concerns arising from that use.

Challenge from Technology

In 1908, Huey (1968) acknowledged that critics had already begun to make predictions that textbooks would be replaced by information that had been presented through a novel technology. With this new technology, "an author may take his thought directly into some sort of gramophone-film book which will render it again to listeners, at will" (p. 429). Huey dismissed these predictions as wild speculations and a year later Dutton and Snedden (1909) agreed that the centrality of textbooks in education was secure. Even so, some critics continued to insist that novel forms of media would replace textbooks. For example, Lindop (1954) described the excitement when radios were

Table 6.2 Criticism of Textbook Pedagogy during the Second Half of the Twentieth Century

"[Along with teachers and buildings,] educators continue to rank the textbook as one of the three major factors in the more formal school curriculum." (Burnett, 1950)

"While some publishers revise their books from cover to cover more often than is necessary, others recopyright old books on the flimsiest of pretexts or no pretext at all." (Knowlton, 1950)

"Many a boy leaves school with an ingrained conviction that all books must be a bore, because the books the school takes most seriously are nothing but a bore." (Mayer, 1962)

"During your child's school career he will attempt to absorb at least 32,000 textbook pages." (Black, 1967)

"Publishing personnel, from editorial to sales, consists of outstanding teachers." (Edgerton, 1969)

"Texts are not 'written' anymore; they are, as the people in the industry say, 'developed,' and this process involves large numbers of people and many compromises." (Fitzgerald, 1979)

"So far in our history, publishers have not caused the large group of educators or citizens to seek other means of obtaining the textbooks and other materials needed in the classroom." (Williamson, 1979)

"Two national surveys have confirmed that teachers use textbooks for more than 70 percent of their instructional time." (Kirst, 1984)

"The problem with too many textbooks today is that they are not bad enough to be bad—they are bad enough to be mediocre." (Remark by an unidentified educator, quoted by Marquand, 1985b)

"The textbook is a timesaver, a prepackaged 'delivery system' that helps conserve teachers' time and energy." (Sewall, 1987)

"The gray utilitarian primer has evolved into a four color visual spectacle that is bigger if not better." (Sewall, 1988)

"Most companies are owned by larger companies, and the executives of those parent companies insist on profit, not academic excellence." (Tyson-Bernstein, 1989)

Continued on next page

Table 6.2 (Continued)

"Textbooks continue to dominate the elementary, middle and secondary curriculum as the major instructional tool." (Ciborowski, 1992)

introduced into 1920s schools. He reported that a group of educators thought that radio-based lessons would soon be broadcast into every classroom. Although this had not transpired after several decades, proponents of radio-based learning were still highlighting the advantages of the popular medium in the 1940s. As one instance, Levenson (1945) advised teachers of the benefits of radio-based learning, such as its potential to help children who were unable to read textbooks.

Radio did not live up to the optimistic forecasts about its educational value. Other innovative technical media fell short of the predictions about their impact as well. For example, support as ardent as that for educational radio had accompanied silent films. This ardor was apparent in World War I advertisements for motion pictures that were to be shown in schools. However, Bagley (1930) observed that silent motion pictures had a negligible influence on education. In agreement, Wise (1939) admitted that film-based education hardly spread in the schools during the period that followed the 1920s. He speculated that educational films would be used frequently only after they could compete with textbooks in arousing interest, stimulating imagination, highlighting details, aiding retention, and giving pleasure.

During the 1950s, many of the educational expectations for radio and film were transferred to television. However, as television's popularity grew, caution about its benefits increased proportionately. After noting that radio, film, and television transmitted trivial and sometimes evil messages as readily as important or moral ones, Good (1956) concluded that textbooks were advantageous because they could be managed more securely than the other media. Nine years later, Frazier (1959) complained about the content of educational television. He thought that even the format for televised educational programs had been conceived so rigidly that the programs had devolved into "talking textbooks." Jennings (1964) also concluded that television had not become an influential, educational medium and speculated that its advancement in the schools might require carefully correlated textbooks.

Having pointed to the educational problems of technologies such as radio, film, and television, some critics expected similar problems with computers. Though problems did develop after their 1970s classroom advent, computer problems were linked primarily to unreliable hardware and inflexible software.

Despite some pessimistic prophecies, the number of computers in the schools increased dramatically during the 1980s. Classroom computers proliferated because they individualized instruction, promoted motivation, and reduced the drudgery of textbook drills. However, the true educational usefulness of classroom computers became apparent during the 1990s with the emergence of the Internet. The Internet was an avenue to inexpensive communication and unlimited information. As a result of the Internet, computers responded decisively to the challenge that Wise (1939) had made a half century earlier, when he had dared any emerging technology that aspired to be successful in the schools to exceed textbooks in arousing interest, retention, and pleasure.

Summary

Early concerns about textbook pedagogy produced changes in print, paper, and spacing. Attention later shifted to more subtle features such as vocabulary and grammar. Publishers also refined the formats of books and even the instructional procedures that they incorporated. As the effectiveness of textbooks increased, some critics worried that the materials were siphoning away teachers' creativity. They also thought that novel media would replace textbooks. Though predictions of obsolescence and denigration persisted throughout the century, textbooks remained the dominant classroom materials.

References

Adams, C. K. (1909). *A history of the United States* (Rev. ed.). New York: Allyn & Bacon.

Alexander, W. W. (1933). Southern white schools study race questions. *Journal of Negro Education, 2*, 139–146.

Allen, H. (1926). The anti-evolution campaign in America. *Current History, 24*, 893–897.

Allen, V. S. (1971). An analysis of textbooks relative to the treatment of Black Americans. *Journal of Negro Education, 40*, 140–145.

American Association of University Women. (1929). *Report of the committee on U.S. history textbooks used in the U.S. schools.* Washington, DC: Author.

———. (1992). *How schools shortchange girls: A study of major findings on girls and education.* Washington, DC: Author/National Education Association.

———. (1999). *Gender gaps: Where schools still fail our children.* New York: Marlowe.

American Council on Education. (1944). *Latin America in school and college teaching materials* (Report of the Committee on the Study of Teaching Materials on Inter-American Subjects). Washington, DC: Author.

———. (1949). *Intergroup relations in teaching materials: A survey and appraisal* (Report of the Committee on the Study of Teaching Materials in Intergroup Relations). Washington, DC: Author.

American Federation of Teachers. (1987). *Democracy's untold story: What would history textbooks neglect.* Washington, DC: Author.

American School Citizenship League. (1921). *Course with type studies, Grade VII: An American citizenship course in United States history.* New York: Scribner's.

Andrews, H. D. (1926). Selecting a textbook. *American School Board Journal, 76*, 67, 152, 154, 157–158.

Anti-Evolution law in Tennessee. (1926, April 9). *Science*, xii–xiv.

Armstrong, L. E. (1911). Apportionment of school funds. *Sierra Educational News, 7* (2), 7–14.

Armstrong, O. K. (1940, September). Treason in the textbooks. *American Legion Magazine, 20* (3), 8–9, 51, 70–72.

Arnold, S. L., & Gilbert, C. B. (1898). *Stepping stones to literature: A reader for higher grades.* New York, Silver, Burdett.

Ashley, R. L. (1907). *American history: For use in secondary schools.* New York: Macmillan.

————. (1915). *American history: For use in secondary schools* (Rev. ed.). New York: Macmillan.

Association for Peace Education. (1923). *An analysis of the emphasis upon war in our elementary school histories [pamphlet]*. Chicago, IL: Author.

Association of History Teachers of the Middle States and Maryland. (1923). History textbooks and truth. *Proceeding of the Association of History Teachers of the Middle States and Maryland, 24*, 26–33.

Avery, L. B. (1919). State-printed textbooks in California. *Elementary School Journal, 19*, 628–633.

Bagley, W. C. (1930). The future of education in America. *Proceedings of the sixty-eighth annual meeting of the National Education Association, 68*, 218–225.

Bainbridge, J. (1952, October). Danger's ahead in the public schools. *McCall's, 56*, 92–94, 98, 108, 110, 112, 116, 120, 122.

Baker, F. T., Carpenter, G. R., & Robbins, I. E. (1906). *Fourth year language reader.* New York: Macmillan.

Banks, J. A. (1969). A content analysis of the Black American in textbooks. *Social Education, 33*, 954–957, 963.

Barber, E. (1975, March 23). Birth of a textbook: Much labor and risk. *New York Times*, p. 16.

Barker, E. C., Dodd, W. E., & Commager, H. S. (1937). *Our nation's development.* New York: Row, Peterson.

Barker, E. C., Webb, W. P., & Dodd, W. E. (1928). *Our nation's development.* New York: Row, Peterson.

Barnard, H. (1863a). American textbooks. *American Journal of Education, 13*, 210–222.

————. (1863b). American textbooks. *American Journal of Education, 13*, 401–408.

————. (1863c). American textbooks. *American Journal of Education, 13*, 626–640.

————. (1864a). American textbooks. *American Journal of Education, 14*, 601–607.

————. (1864b). American textbooks. *American Journal of Education, 14*, 753–778.

————. (1865). American school books. *American Journal of Education, 15*, 539–575.

Bates, H. (Ed.). (1906). *Palgrave's the golden treasury.* New York: Longmans, Green.

Battle over evolution spreads to Kansas; Friends burn school's "Book of Knowledge." (1925, May 28). *New York Times*, p. 8.

Beale, H. K. (1936). *Are American teachers free? An analysis of restraints upon the freedom of teaching in American schools* (Report of the Commission on the Social Studies, Part 12). New York: Scribner's.

Beauchamp, W. L., Williams, M. M., & Blough, G. O. (1948). *Discovering our world: Book 3*. Chicago: Scott, Foresman.

Beaver, W. C. (1958). *General biology* (5th ed.). St. Louis, MO: Mosby.

Beechold, H. F. (1971). *The creative classroom: Teaching without textbooks*. New York: Scribner's.

Black, H. (1967, October 7). What our children read. *Saturday Evening Post, 240* (20), 27–29, 72–79, 82.

Blanshard, P. (1955). *The right to read: The battle against censorship*. Boston: Beacon.

Bode, B. H. (1928, January 11). On the use of textbooks. *Ohio State University Educational Research Bulletin*, 10–11.

Book publishing: As simple as ABC. (1987, June 22). *Fortune, 115* (113), 9–10.

Bowler, M. (1978). The making of a textbook. *Learning, 6* (7), 38–42.

Bragdon, H. W. (1969). Dilemmas of a textbook writer. *Social Education, 33*, 292–298.

Brammer, M. (1967). Textbook publishing. In C. B. Grannis (Ed.), *What happens in book publishing* (2nd ed., pp. 320–349). New York: Columbia University Press.

Broome, E. C., & Adams, E. W. (1935). *Conduct and citizenship* (Rev. ed.). New York: Macmillan.

Broudy, E. (1975). The trouble with textbooks. *Teachers College Record, 77*, 13–34.

Brown, G. E. (1915). Should the state publish its own textbooks. *Journal of Education, 81*, 566–567.

Brown, J. F. (1915a). *State publication of school books*. New York: Macmillan.

———. (1915b). State publication of school books. *School and Society, 2*, 474–485.

———. (1919). Textbooks and publishers. *Elementary School Journal, 19*, 382–388.

Bruce, W. G., & Bruce, W. C. (1925). The state publication of school books. *American School Board Journal, 71* (3), 67.

Burkhardt, R. W. (1946). The Far East in modern problems and civics tests [*sic*]. In American Council on Education (Ed.), *Treatment of Asia in American textbooks* (pp. 79–104). New York: American Council, Institute of Pacific Relations.

———. (1947–1948, winter edition). The Soviet Union in American school textbooks. *Public Opinion Quarterly, 11,* 567–571.

Burnett, L. W. (1950). Textbook provisions in the several states. *Journal of Educational Research, 43,* 357–366.

———. (1952). State textbook policies. *Phi Delta Kappan, 33,* 257–261.

Burnham, S. (1920). *The making of our country: A history of the United States for schools.* Chicago: Winston.

Burnham, W. H., Small, W. S., & Standish, M. (1911). Report of the committee on the standardization of school books, etc. *American Physical Education Review, 16,* 254–257.

Burr, E., Dunn, S., & Farquhar, N. (1972). Women and the language of inequality. *Social Education, 36,* 841–845.

Bushnell, A. (1911). *School books and international prejudices* (Monograph No. 38). New York: American Association for International Conciliation.

Butcher, T. W. (1919). Some difficulties attending the work of a textbook commission. *Elementary School Journal, 19,* 500–505.

Butterfield, R. A., Demos, E. S., Grant, W. W., Moy, P. S., & Perez, A. L. (1979). A multicultural analysis of a popular basal reading series in the international year of the child. *Journal of Negro Education, 48,* 382–389.

Calvert, R. C. (1932). *The new first course in home making.* Atlanta, GA: Smith, Hammond.

Canfield, L. H., Wilder, H. B., Paxson, F. L., Coulter, E. M., & Mead, N. P. (1938). *The United States in the making.* Boston: Houghton Mifflin.

Capen, L. I., & Melchior, D. M. (1937). *My worth to the world: Studies in citizenship.* New York: American.

Capitol Hill—Faggots on the fire. (1953, June 29). *New Republic, 128,* 10–11.

Carle, E. (1972). *The hate factory.* Fullerton, CA: Educator.

Carpenter, M. E. (1941). *The treatment of the Negro in American history school textbooks: A comparison of changing textbook content, 1826 to 1839, with developing scholarship in the history of the Negro in the United States.* Menasha, WI: Banta.

Carroll, C. F., & Brooks, S. C. (1906). *The Brooks primer.* New York: Appleton.

Cast, G. C. (1919). Selecting text-books. *Elementary School Journal, 19,* 468–472.

Chall, J. S., & Conard, S. S. (1991). *Should textbooks challenge students? The case for easier or harder textbooks.* New York: Teachers College Press.

Chancellor, W. E. (1913). The state publication question. *School Journal, 80,* 218–220.

Channing, E. (1905). *A student's history of the United States* (Rev. ed.). New York: Macmillan.

———. (1908). *A student's history of the United States* (Rev. ed.). New York: Macmillan.

Chase, W. L., & Cornforth, M. C. (1932). The world war in junior high school history textbooks. *Education, 53,* 224–228.

Child, I. L., Potter, E. H., & Levine, E. M. (1946). *Children's textbooks and personality development: An exploration in the social psychology of education* (Psychological Monograph No. 279). Washington, DC: American Psychological Association.

Ciborowski, J. (1992). *Textbooks and the students who can't read them: A guide to teaching content.* Brookline, MA: Brookline.

Clyse, J. (1959). What do basic readers teach about jobs? *Elementary School Journal, 59,* 456–460.

Coffman, L. D. (1919). Should authors be concerned with the method of distribution of textbooks? *Proceedings of the National Education Association, 57,* 468–469.

Cohen, O. (1970). Preface. In M. B. Kane, *Minorities in textbooks: A study of their treatment in social studies texts* (pp. i–iv). Chicago: Anti-Defamation League of B'nai B'rith.

Cole, C. E. (1939). The war contents of American history textbooks. *Social Studies, 30,* 195–197.

Coleman, C. H., & Wesley, E. B. (1939). *America's road to now.* Boston: Heath.

Compton, M. A. (1932). An evaluation of history texts: A check list. *Historical Outlook, 23,* 277–287.

Condon, R. J. (1928). *Outward bound.* Boston: Little, Brown.

Conlan, J. B. (1976). Foreword. In J. C. Hefley. *Textbooks on trial* (pp. 5–7). Wheaton, IL: Victor.

Conn, H. (1978). *Four Trojan horses.* Nyack, NY: Parson.

Cook, W. A. (1927). *Federal and state school administration.* New York: Crowell.

Cornell, L. S. (1888). State uniformity of textbooks. *Addresses and Proceedings of the National Education Association, 28,* 225–233.

Counts, G. S. (1946). Soviet version of American history. *Public Opinion Quarterly, 10,* 321–328.

Cox, E. M. (1903). Free text-books. *Western Journal of Education, 8,* 88–98.

Crissey, F. (1912, December 14). Expensive free education: An interview with the president of the Illinois Federation of Labor. *Saturday Evening Post,* 14–15, 29.

Criticism of Kansas textbook publication. (1917). *Elementary School Journal, 17*, 537–541.

Crumpton, C. E. (1928). *Junior high school English: Book one.* New York: American.

Cubberly, E. P. (1926). A distinctive American achievement. *Educational Progress, 5* (2), 4–5.

Cyr, E. M. (1899a). *Cyr's fifth reader.* Boston: Ginn.

————. (1899b). *Cyr's fourth reader.* Boston: Ginn.

Dahlin, R. (1981, August 7). A tough time for textbooks. *Publishers Weekly, 215*, 28–32.

Darling, E. (1954). *How we fought for our schools: A documentary novel.* New York: Norton.

Darling, M. S., & Greenberg, B. B. (1937). *Effective citizenship: Personal, vocational, and community civics.* New York: Prentice-Hall.

Davidson, C. (1953, June 29). St. Cloud—How the flames spread. *New Republic, 128*, 13–14.

Davis, B. (1985, January 3). Many forces shape marking and marketing of a new schoolbook: Houghton Mifflin consulted teachers and minorities before publishing a text—Approval from a feminist. *Wall Street Journal*, pp. 1, 8.

Davis, N. S. (1920). *Vocational arithmetic for girls.* Milwaukee, WI: Bruce.

Davis, P. R. (1930). *State publication of textbooks in California.* Berkeley, CA: California Society of Secondary Education.

Davis-Dubois, R. (1935). Our enemy: The stereotype. *Progressive Education, 12*, 146–150.

Decision for liberty. (1923). *School and Society, 17*, 668–669.

Dessauer, J. P. (1976, July 26). Economic review of the book industry: A special *Publishers Weekly* feature. *Publishers Weekly, 210*, 35.

Dewey, H. B. (1920). Textbook legislation—Its inconsistencies and injustice—The remedy. *American School Board Journal, 60*, 31–32.

Dexter, E. G. (1904). *A history of education in the United States.* New York: Macmillan.

Dill, B. E. (1921). How to improve textbooks—Sensing the demand. *Proceedings of the National Education Association, 59*, 421–425.

Donovan. H. L. (1924). How to select textbooks. *Peabody Journal of Education, 2* (1), 1–11.

Doughton, I. (1917). Choosing textbooks. *American School Board Journal, 55*, 29–30.

Douglas, C. E. (1924). Educating the public to higher standards of textbook making. *Addresses and Proceedings of the National Education Association, 62*, 537–541.

Dryer, C. R. (1912). *High school geography: Physical, economic, and regional.* New York: American.

Duncan, H. (1979). *Secular humanism: The most dangerous religion in America.* Lubbock, TX: Missionary Crusader.

Dutton, S. T., & Snedden, D. (1909). *The administration of public education in the United States.* New York: Macmillan.

Eagleton, C. (1918). Discussion: The attitude of our textbooks toward England. *Education Review, 56*, 424–429.

Economizing in text-books. (1918). *School and Society, 8*, 294.

Edgerton, R. B. (1969). Odyssey of a book: How a social studies text comes into being. *Social Education, 33*, 279–286.

Edmonson, J. B., & Dondineau, A. (1927). *Citizenship through problems: For junior high school grades.* New York: Macmillan.

Elkin, S. M. (1965). Minorities in textbooks: The latest chapter. *Teachers College Record, 66*, 502–508.

Ellington, L. (1986). Blacks and Hispanics in high school economics texts. *Social Education, 50*, 64–66.

Elliott, D. L. (1990). Textbooks and the curriculum in the postwar era: 1950–1980. In D. L. Elliott & A. Woodward (Eds.), *Textbooks and schooling in the United States* (89th Yearbook of the National Society for the Study of Education, Part I, pp. 42–55). Chicago, IL: University of Chicago Press.

Elson, H. W. (1941). *History of the United States of America* (Rev. ed.). New York: Macmillan.

Emerson, H. P., & Bender, I. C. (1915). *English spoken and written—Primer: Lessons in language for primary grades.* New York: Macmillan.

England, J. M. (1963). England and America in the schoolbooks of the Republic, 1783–1861. *University of Birmingham Historical Journal, 9*, 92–111.

English, R. (1980). The politics of textbook adoption. *Phi Delta Kappan, 62*, 275–278.

Evans, L. B. (1914). State publication of textbooks. *School and Home, 6* (6), 7–10.

Evolution in education in California. (1925). *Science, 61*, 367–368.

Facts about school book costs: An interview with the manager of a leading text-book house. (March, 1913). *American School Board Journal, 46*, 13–14, 52.

Fang, I. E. (1967). The "easy listening formula." *Journal of Broadcasting, 11* (1), 63–68.

Faulkner, H. U., Kepner, T., & Bartlett, H. (1941). *The American way of life: A history.* New York: Harper.

Faulkner, R. D. (1900). The California state text-book system. *Educational Review, 20,* 44–60.

Fehlau, U. E. (1961). *Fundamental German* (2nd ed.). New York: Harper.

Feminists on Children's Literature [Committee]. (1971). A feminist look at children's books. *Library Journal, 96,* 253–240.

Fish, C. R. (1927). *Teachers' manual for "History of America."* New York: American.

Fishman, A. S. (1976). A criticism of sexism in elementary readers. *Reading Teacher, 29,* 443–446.

Fiske, J. (1899). *A history of the United States for schools.* Boston: Houghton Mifflin.

Fite, E. D. (1919). *History of the United States* (2nd ed.). New York: Holt.

Fitzgerald, F. (1979). *America revised: History schoolbooks in the twentieth century.* Boston: Little, Brown.

Fitzpatrick, F. A. (1912). The bookman in his relation to the textbook problem. *Education Review, 43,* 282–291.

Fitzpatrick, F. L., & Horton, R. E. (1935). *Biology.* Boston: Houghton Mifflin.

Fleming, D. (1981). The impact of nationalism on world geography textbooks in the United States. *International Journal of Political Education, 4,* 373–381.

Flynn, J. T. (1951, October). Who owns your child's mind? *Reader's Digest, 59* (10), 23–28.

Follett, R. (1985). The school textbook adoption process. *Book Research Quarterly, 1,* 19–22.

Forman, S. E. (1919). *Advanced American history.* New York: Century.

Fowlkes, J. G. (1923). *Evaluating school textbooks.* New York: Silver, Burdett.

Fox, T. E., & Hess, R. D. (1972). *An analysis of social conflict in social studies textbooks.* Washington, DC: U.S. Office of Education.

Fox, W. (1985, December 1). Textbook publishing is profitable but controlled. *Boston Sunday Globe,* p. 28.

Frazier, A. (1959). We need more than talking textbooks. In A. Frazier & H. E. Wigren (Eds.), *Opportunities for learning: Guidelines for television* (pp. 42–45). Washington, DC: National Education Association.

Freeland, G. E., Walker, E. E., & Williams, H. E. (1937). *America's building: The makers of our flag.* New York: Scribner's.

Fry, E. (1968). A readability formula that saves time. *Journal of Reading, 11*, 513–516, 575–578.

Gabler, M., & Gabler, N. (1982). Mind control through textbooks. *Phi Delta Kappan, 64*, 96.

Gestie, B. D. (1937). The revision of text-books to avoid international misunderstanding. *School and Society, 46*, 709–714.

Gilliland, A. R. (1923). The effect on reading of changes in the size of type. *Elementary School Journal, 24*, 138–146.

Ginn, E. (1910). The school book, the publisher and the public. *Independent, 69*, 222–225.

Giordano, G. (2000). *Twentieth century reading education: The era of remedial reading.* Stamford, CT: JAI.

Glazer, N., & Ueda, R. (1983). *Ethnic groups in history textbooks.* Washington, DC: Ethics and Public Policy Center.

Good, H. G. (1956). *A history of American education.* New York: Macmillan.

Goodrich, S. G. (1839). *The third reader for the use of schools.* Louisville, KY: Morton and Griswold.

Gordy, W. F. (1925). *History of the United States.* New York: Scribner's.

Gould, S. J. (1999). *Rocks of ages: Science and religion in the fullness of life.* New York: Balantine.

Graebner, D. B. (1972). A decade of sexism in readers. *Reading Teacher, 26*, 52–58.

Graham, A. (1986). Elementary social studies texts: An author-editor's viewpoint. *Social Education, 50*, 54–55.

Grambs, J. D. (1970). Instructional materials for the disadvantaged child. In A. H. Passow (Ed.), *Reaching the disadvantaged learner* (pp. 167–182). New York: Teachers College Press.

Green, A. (1926). The measurement of modern language books. *Modern Language Journal, 10*, 259–269.

Griffen, W., & Marciano, J. (1980). Vietnam   The textbook version. *Social Science Record, 17*, 16–20.

Griffing, H., & Franz, S. I. (1896). On the conditions of fatigue in reading. *Psychological Review, 3*, 513–520.

Hahn, C. L., & Blankenship, G. (1983). Women and economics textbooks. *Theory and Research in Social Education, 11* (3), 67–76.

Hall-Quest, A. L. (1920). *The textbook: How to use and judge it.* New York: Macmillan.

Hamm, W. A. (1938). *The American people.* Boston: Heath.

Harbourt, J. (1931). The world war in French, German, English, and American secondary school textbooks (*Yearbook of the National Council for the Social Studies*, Vol. 1, pp. 54–117). Arlington, VA: National Council for the Social Studies.

Harding, S. B. (1919). What the war should do for our history methods. *Historical Outlook, 10,* 189–190.

Harman, R. V., Tucker, H. R., & Wrench, J. E. (1926). *American citizenship practice.* Lincoln, NE: University Publishing.

Harris, J. J. (1963). *The treatment of religion in elementary school social studies textbooks.* New York: Anti-Defamation League of B'nai B'rith.

Harris, W. T. (1914). The importance of the textbook. *Journal of Education, 80,* 317.

Harrison, L., & Passero, R. N. (1975). Sexism in the language of elementary school textbooks. *Science and Children, 12* (1), 22–25.

Hart, A. B. (1921). *New American history.* New York: American.

Hart, D. V. (1944). What do our school books say about Latin America? *Harvard Educational Review, 14,* 210–220.

Hart, J. K. (1924). *Social life and institutions: An elementary study of society.* Yonkers-on-Hudson, New York: World.

————. (1937). *An introduction to the social studies: An elementary textbook for professional and preparatory groups.* New York: Macmillan.

Hayes, C. J. H. (1923). Nationalism and the social studies. *Historical Outlook, 14,* 247–250.

Hays, A. G. (1925, August 5). The strategy of the Scopes defense. *Nation, 121,* 157–158.

Hechinger, F. M. (1960, February 14). High school history textbooks play it safe by avoiding the tough issues. *New York Times,* p. E-9.

Hefley, J. C. (1976). *Textbooks on trial.* Wheaton, IL: Victor.

Hepner, W. R., & Hepner, F. K. (1924). *The good citizen: A textbook in social and vocational civics.* Boston: Houghton Mifflin.

Hershey, J. (1954, May 24). Why do students bog down on first "r"? *Life, 36,* 136–140, 142, 144, 147–148.

Herzberg, M. J. (1917). Ten rules in the choice of textbooks. *American School Board Journal, 74,* 26, 42.

Hicks, J. D. (1949). *A short history of American democracy.* Boston: Houghton Mifflin.

Higbee, E. E. (1888). Discussion—State uniformity of textbooks. *Addresses and Proceedings of the National Education Association, 28,* 229–233.

Hillocks, G. (1978). Books and bombs: Ideological conflict and the schools—A case study of the Kanawha County book protest. *School Review, 86,* 632–654.

Hilton, H. H. (1913). Cost of textbooks per pupil. *Journal of Education, 77,* 369.

Hofstadter, R., Miller, W., & Aaron, D. (1957). *The United States: The history of a republic.* Englewood Cliffs, NJ: Prentice-Hall.

Hood, W. R. (1922). *Some important school legislation, 1921 and 1922.* (U.S. Bureau of Education Bulletin, 1922, No. 43). Washington, DC: Government Printing Office.

———. (1923). *The Bible in the public schools: Legal status and current practice* (U.S. Bureau of Education Bulletin, 1923, No. 15). Washington, DC: Government Printing Office.

Horn, E. (1922). Introduction. In R. H. Franzen & F. B. Knight, *Textbook selection* (pp. 5–8). Baltimore: Warwick.

Howley, M. C. (1959). *The treatment of religion in American history textbooks for grades seven and eight from 1783 to 1956.* Unpublished doctoral dissertation, Teachers College—Columbia University, New York.

Huey, E. B. (1900). On the psychology and physiology of reading—I. *American Journal of Psychology, 11,* 283–302.

———. (1968). *The psychology and pedagogy of reading: With a review of the history of reading and writing and of methods, texts, and hygiene in reading.* Cambridge, MA: MIT. (Original work published in 1908)

Hughes, R. O. (1948). *Today's problems.* Boston: Allyn & Bacon.

Hunt, E. M. (1947). The relation of American history to the other social studies. In R. E. Thursfield (Ed.), *The study and teaching of American history* (pp. 173–204). Washington, DC: National Council for the Social Studies.

Hunter, G. W. (1907). *Elements of biology: A practical text-book correlating botany, zoölogy, and human physiology.* New York: American.

Huntington, E., Williams, F. E., Brown, R. M., & Chase, L. E. (1922). *Business geography.* New York: Wiley.

Integrating the texts. (1966, March 7). *Newsweek, 67,* 93–94.

International Institute of Intellectual Co-operation. (1933). *School text-book revision and international understanding* (2nd ed.). Paris: League of Nations.

Is this the end to the Scopes case? (1927, January 27). *Christian Century, 44,* 100.

Jacobs, W. J. (1983, March 30). Whose textbooks are they, anyway? —Remembering the legacy of Meletus. *Education Week, 2* (4), 24.

Janis, J. (1970). Textbook revisions in the sixties. *Teachers College Record, 72,* 289–301.

Jenks, J. W. (1906). *Citizenship and the schools.* New York: Holt.

Jennings, F. G. (1964, January 18). Textbooks and trapped idealists. *Saturday Review, 47,* 57–59, 77–78.

Jensen, F. A. (1931). The selection of manuscripts by publishers. In G. M. Whipple (Ed.), *The textbook in American education* (30th Yearbook of the National Society for the Study of Education, Part II, pp. 79–92). Bloomington, IL: Public School Publishing.

Johnson, C. (1904). More quaint readers in the old-time school. *New England Magazine, 24,* 626–637.

Johnson, F. W. (1925). A checking list for the selection of high school textbooks. *Teachers College Record, 27,* 104–108.

Johnson, G. R. (1930). An objective method of determining reading difficulty. *Journal of Educational Research, 21,* 283–287.

Joint Committee of the National Education Association and Association of American Publishers. (1972). *Selecting instructional materials for purchase: Procedural guidelines.* Washington, DC: National Education Association.

Jones, C. F., & Darkenwald, G. G. (1941). *Economic geography.* New York: Macmillan.

Jones, E. S. (1935). *Practice handbook in English: A drilllbook and review in the essentials of writing and speaking.* New York: Appleton-Century.

Judd, C. H. (1918). Analyzing text-books. *Elementary School Journal, 19,* 143–154.

Kane, M. B. (1970). *Minorities in textbooks: A study of their treatment in social studies texts.* Chicago: Anti-Defamation League of B'nai B'rith.

Kansas decision on textbooks. (1913). *Elementary School Teacher, 13,* 414–415.

Kealey, R. J. (1980). The image of the family in second-grade readers. *Momentum, 11* (9), 16–19.

Kelsey, R. W. (1921). History teaching in Germany. *Historical Outlook, 12,* 153–157.

Kendig-Gill, I. (1923). *War and peace in United States history text-books* [pamphlet]. Washington, DC: National Council for Prevention of War.

Kimball, L. G. (1900). *The structure of the English sentence.* New York: American.

Kinne, H., & Cooley, A. M. (1917). *The home and the family: An elementary textbook of home making.* New York: Macmillan.

Kirp, D. L., (1991). Textbooks and tribalism in California. *Public Interest, 104,* 20–36.

Kirst, M. W. (1984). Choosing textbooks: Reflections of a state board president. *American Educator, 8* (2), 18–23.

Knight, E. W. (1949). Southern opposition to northern education. *Educational Forum, 14*, 47–58.

———. (1952). *Fifty years of American education, 1900–1950: A historical review and critical appraisal.* New York: Ronald.

Knowlton, D. C. (1925). The teaching of history in the junior high school: Tools and workroom. *Historical Outlook, 16* (2), 76–79.

———. (1926). *History and the other social studies in the junior high school.* New York: Scribner's Sons.

Knowlton, D. C., & Harden, M. (1938). *Our America: Past and present.* New York: American.

Knowlton, P. A. (1950). What is wrong with textbooks? *School Executive, 70* (2), 56–58.

Koopman, H. L. (1909a). Scientific tests of type. *Printing Art, 8*, 81–83.

———. (1909b). Types and eyes. *Printing Art, 7*, 359–361.

Kretman, K. P., & Parker, B. (1986). New U.S. history texts: Good news and bad. *Social Education, 50*, 61–63.

Krug, M. M. (1960). "Safe" textbooks and citizenship education. *School Review, 68*, 463–480.

———. (1963). The distant cousins: A comparative study of selected history textbooks in England and the United States. *School Review, 71*, 425–441.

Langton, K. P., & Jennings, M. K. (1968). Political socialization and the high school civics curriculum in the United States. *American Political Science Review, 62*, 852–867.

Lauwerys, J. A. (1953). *History textbooks and international understanding.* Paris: UNESCO.

Law, F. H. (1927). *English for immediate use: With drill in essentials.* New York: Scribner's.

Lehmann Haupt, H., Wroth, L. C., & Silver, R. G. (1951). *The book in America* (2nd ed.). New York: Bowker.

Leighton, F. (1928). Changes in textbooks: How Oswego, N.Y., enlists the aid of the teachers. *American School Board Journal, 78*, 39, 134.

Leo, J. (1999, February 22). Gender wars redux. *U.S. News & World Report, 126* (7), 24.

Lerner, R., Nagai, A. K., & Rothman, S. (1989). Filler feminism in high school history. *Academic Questions, 5* (1), 28–40.

Lerner, R., & Rothman, S. (1990, April). Newspeak, feminist-style. *Commentary*, *89*, 54–56.

Levenson, W. B. (1945). *Teaching through radio*. New York: Farrar & Rinehart.

Levine, M. (1937). Social problems in American history textbooks. *Social Studies*, *28*, 161–166.

Lew, T. T. (1923). *China in American school text-books: A problem of education in international understanding and worldwide brotherhood* (Special Supplement of the Chinese Social and Political Science Review). Peking, China: Chinese Social and Political Science Association.

Lichter, J. H., & Johnson, D. W. (1969). Changes in attitudes toward Negroes of white elementary school students after use of multiethnic readers. *Journal of Educational Psychology*, *60*, 148–152.

Lindop, B. E. (1954). Radio education in historical perspective. In J. S. Kinder & F. D. McClusky (Eds.), *Audio-visual reader* (pp. 122–127). Dubuque, IA: Brown.

Lively, B. A., & Pressey, S. L. (1923). A method for measuring the "vocabulary burden" of textbooks. *Educational Administration and Supervision*, *9*, 389–398.

Lutz, P. E. (1929). Nationalism in German history textbooks after the war. *Historical Outlook*, *20*, 273–279.

Madison, C. A. (1966). *Book publishing in America*. New York: McGraw-Hill.

Man—Memo from a publisher. (1974, October 20), *New York Times*, pp. 38, 104–108.

Marcus, L. (1961). *The treatment of minorities in secondary school textbooks*. New York: B'nai B'rith.

Margolis, R. J. (1965). The well-tempered textbook. *Education Digest*, *31* (4), 24–27.

Marquand, R. (1985a, October 25). Textbook maker's view: The ground rules need to be changed. *Christian Science Monitor*, p. B7.

———. (1985b, October 25). Textbooks: Debate heats up over the growing push for reform. *Christian Science Monitor*, pp. B1, B5–B6.

Marshall, W. I. (1895). *Should the public schools furnish text-books free to all pupils?* Chicago: Illinois State Teachers' Association.

Marten, L. A., & Matlin, M. W. (1976). Does sexism in elementary readers still exist? *Reading Teacher*, *29*, 764–767.

Marwick, W. F., & Smith, W. A. (1900). *The true citizen: How to become one*. New York: American.

Massialas, B. G. (1961). Selecting a social studies textbook. *Social Education*, *25*, 237–238.

————. (1963). Revising the social studies: An inquiry-centered approach. *Social Education, 27*, 185–189.

Mathews, J. B. (1953). Reds and our churches. *American Mercury, 77* (1), 3–13.

Mavor, J. W. (1937). *General biology.* New York: Macmillan.

Maxwell, C. R. (1921). *The selection of textbooks.* Boston: Houghton Mifflin.

Mayer, M. (1962, July). The trouble with textbooks. *Harper's Magazine, 225*, 65–71.

McCray, D. O. (1914). Kansas wise and otherwise. *Journal of Education, 80*, 200–202.

McCullough, J. F. (1922). *Looking to our foundations.* Geneva, IL: Economic.

McDonald, S. M. (1989). Sex bias in the representation of male and female characters in children's picture books. *Journal of Genetic Psychology, 150*, 389–401.

McGregor, F. H. (1908, April). Free text books. *American School Board Journal, 36*, 27.

McGuffey, W. H. (1920). *McGuffey's first eclectic reader* (Rev. ed.). New York: American.

McKeon, R., Merton, R. K., & Gelhorn, W. (1957). *The freedom to read: Perspective and program.* New York: Bowker.

McLaurin, M. (1971). Images of Negroes in deep South public school state history texts. *Phylon, 32*, 237–246.

McMaster, J. B. (1916). *A brief history of the United States* (Rev. ed.). New York: American.

McMurray, F., & Cronbach, L. J. (1955). The controversial past and present of the text. In L. J. Cronbach (Ed.), *Text materials in modern education* (pp. 9–27). Urbana, IL: University of Illinois Press.

McNeal, T. A. (1915). Discussion and correspondence: The state publication of school books. *School and Society, 2*, 669–670.

Mead, C. D. (1918). The best method of selecting text-books. *Educational Administration and Supervision, 4* (2), 61–69.

Middleton, G. (1911). The text-book game and its quarry. *Bookman, 33*, 141–147.

Miller, A. M. (1922). Kentucky and the theory of evolution. *Science, 55*, 178–180.

Miller, F. M. (1916). *History in story, song and action* (Vol. 2). Boston: Educational Publishing.

Monahan, J. (1915). *Free textbooks and state uniformity* (U.S. Bureau of Education Bulletin No. 36). Washington, DC: Government Printing Office.

Montgomery, D. H. (1905). *The student's American history* (Rev. ed.). New York: Ginn.

Moore, C. B. (1936). *Our American citizenship*. New York: Scribner's.

Morgan, J. W. (1860). Our school books. *Debow's Review, 27*, 434–440.

Morris, H. M. (1963). *The twilight of evolution*. Grand Rapids, MI: Baker.

Morse, A. D. (1951, September). Who's trying to ruin our schools? *McCalls, 79*, 26–27, 94, 102, 108–109.

Mowry, W. A., & Mowry, A. M. (1897). *A history of the United States for Schools: Including a concise account of the discovery of America, the colonization of the land, and the Revolutionary War*. New York: Silver, Burdett.

Muzzey, D. S. (1911). *An American history*. Boston: Ginn.

Nation—Scattered alarms. (1953, June 29). *New Republic, 128*, 17.

National Association for the Advancement of Colored People. (1939). *Anti-Negro propaganda in school textbooks*. New York: Author

National Association of Secondary-School Principals. (1949). Curriculum in intergroup relations: Case studies in instruction for secondary schools. *Bulletin of the National Association of Secondary-School Principals, 33* (160), 1–169.

National Education Association. (1937). Improving social studies instruction *National Education Association Research Bulletin, 15*, 188–255.

National Project on Women in Education. (1978). *Taking sexism out of education*. Washington, DC: U.S. Department of Health, Education, and Welfare.

Nelkin, D. (1976). The science-textbook controversies. *Scientific American, 234* (4), 33–39.

Nelson, J., & Roberts, G. (1963). *The censors and the schools*. Boston: Little, Brown.

Nevins, A. (1947, February 23). To take the poison out of textbooks. *New York Times* (magazine section), pp. 7, 63–64.

New York bill on history text-books. (1923, March 31). *School and Society, 17*, 349.

Nichols, A. S., & Ochoa, A. (1971). Evaluating textbooks for elementary social studies: Criteria for the seventies. *Social Education, 35*, 290–294.

Nida, W. L. (1924). *Following the frontier: Stories of the westward movement*. New York: Macmillan.

Nilsen, A. P. (1971). Women in children's literature. *College English, 32*, 918–926.

Noah, H. J., Prince, C. E., & Riggs, C. R. (1962). History in high-school textbooks: A Note. *School Review, 70*, 415–436.

Noble, J. K. (1976, July 26). Book industry stocks: Past, present and prospects. *Publishers Weekly, 210,* 49–50.

Nolen, E. W. (1942). The colored child in contemporary literature. *Horn Book, 18,* 348–355.

Nordberg, W. W. (1976, July 26). Economic events in 1975 and their impact on book demand. *Publishers Weekly, 210,* 36–39.

O'Brien, S. (1988). The reshaping of history: Marketers vs. authors—Who wins? Who loses? *Curriculum Review, 28* (1), 11–14.

O'Donnel, R. W. (1973). Sex bias in primary social studies textbooks. *Educational Leadership, 31,* 137–141.

Ohler, G. W. (1924). Safe economies consistent with improved standards of textbook making. *Addresses and Proceedings of the National Education Association, 60,* 804–808.

O'Rourke, L. J. (1938). *You and your community.* New York: Heath.

Osborn, J., & Stein, M. (1985). Basal reading program: Development, effectiveness, and selection. *Book Research Quarterly, 1* (2), 38–48.

Ostheimer, A. L., & Delaney, J. P. (1945). *Christian principles and national problems.* New York: Sadlier.

Otis, E. M. (1923). A textbook score card. *Journal of Educational Research, 7,* 132–136.

Palsey, J. L. (1987, April 27). Not-so-good books: Whatever happened to Squanto? *New Republic, 196* (17), 20–22.

Parker, J. C., Patterson, C. P., & McAlister, S. B. (1939). *Citizenship in our democracy.* New York: Heath.

Patty, W. W., & Painter, W. I. (1931). Improving our method of selecting high-school textbooks. *Journal of Educational Research, 24,* 23–32.

Peck, E. S. (1923). Textbook democracy. *Education, 43,* 566–569.

Perpiñan, J. E. (1934). The Philippine Islands in American school textbooks. *Journal of Experimental Education, 2,* 366–393.

Pflug, H. A. (1955). Religion in Missouri textbooks. *Phi Delta Kappan, 36,* 258–260.

Pieper, C. J., Beauchamp, W. L., & Frank, O. D. (1934). *Teacher's guidebook for "Everyday Problems in Biology."* Chicago: Scott, Foresman.

———. (1936). *Everyday problems in biology.* Chicago: Scott, Foresman.

Pierce, B. L. (1929). Propaganda in teaching the social studies. *Historical Outlook, 20,* 387–389.

———. (1930). *Civic attitudes in American school textbooks.* Chicago: University of Chicago Press.

————. (1934). The school and the spirit of nationalism. *Annals of the American Academy of Political and Social Science, 175,* 117–122.

Pollard, R. S. (1892). *Pollard's synthetic third reader.* Chicago: Western.

Pooley, R. C., & Walcott, F. G. (1942). *Action!—Growth in Reading, Book 1.* Chicago: Scott, Foresman.

Prescott, D. A. (1930). *Education and international relations: A study of the social forces that determine the influence of education.* Cambridge, MA: Harvard University Press.

Price, R. D. (1966). Textbook dilemma in the social studies. *Social Studies, 57,* 21–23, 26–27.

Prince, J. T. (1910). *A practical English grammar: For upper grades.* Boston: Ginn.

Proposed legislation against the teaching of evolution. (1922). *Science, 55,* 318–320.

Purcell, P., & Stewart, L. (1990). Dick and Jane in 1989. *Sex Roles, 22,* 177–185.

Quality and cost of textbooks. (1915). *Journal of Education, 81,* 681–683.

Ravitch, D., & Finn, C. E. (1987). *What do our 17-year-olds know?* (Report on the First National Assessment of History and Literature). New York: Harper & Row.

Reddick, L. K. (1934). Racial attitudes in American history: Textbooks of the South. *Journal of Negro History, 19,* 225–265.

Redding, M. F. (1963). *Revolution in the textbook publishing industry* (Technological Development Project, Occasional Paper No. 9). Washington, DC: National Education Association.

Reed, A., & Kellogg, B. (1905). *Higher lessons in English: A work on English grammar and composition, in which the science of the language is made tributary to the art of expression—A course of practical lessons carefully graded, and adapted to every-day use in the school-room* (Rev. ed.). New York: Maynard, Merrill.

Reese, L. (1994, Winter). Gender equity and texts. *Social Studies Review, 33,* 12–15.

Reese, L. W. (1928). The textbook company representative. *Michigan Education Journal, 10,* 113.

Reid, J. M. (1969). *An adventure in textbooks: 1924–1960.* New York: Bowker.

Reynolds, C. J. (1952). Textbooks and immigrants. *Phi Delta Kappan, 33,* 295–296.

Richey, H. G. (1931). The professional status of textbook authors. In G. M. Whipple (Ed.), *The textbook in American education* (30th Yearbook of the

National Society for the Study of Education, Part II, pp. 67–78). Bloomington, IL: Public School Publishing.

Robinson, R. R. (1930). *Two centuries of change in the content of school readers*. Nashville, TN: Peabody College.

Root, E. M. (1959). *Brainwashing in the high school: An examination of eleven American history textbooks*. New York: Deven-Adair.

Rosenberg, M. (1972a). Criteria for evaluating the treatment of minority groups in textbooks and other curriculum materials. *Audiovisual Instruction, 17* (11), 21–22.

———. (1972b). Textbooks: Do they meet fair minority group standards? *Educational Leadership, 30*, 141–143.

Ross, E. A. (1932). *Civic sociology: A textbook in social and civic problems for young Americans* (Rev. ed.). Yonkers-on-Hudson, New York: World.

Rothman, R. (1989, December 6). Critics warn mergers in textbook industry could hurt quality. *Education Week, 9*, pp. 1, 12.

Rout, L. (1979, September 5). Revised texts: School history books, striving to please all, are criticized as bland. *Wall Street Journal*, pp. 1, 28.

Rovenger, J. (1983). A matter of bias. *School Library Journal, 29* (9), 34–35.

Roy, R. L. (1953). *Apostles of discord: A study of organized bigotry and disruption on the fringes of Protestantism*. Boston: Beacon.

Rugg, H. (1930). *Changing civilizations in the modern world: A textbook in world geography with historical backgrounds*. Boston: Ginn.

Rundell, W. (1965). History teaching: A legitimate concern. *Social Education, 29*, 521–524, 528.

Russell, W. F. (1914a). Early methods in teaching history in secondary schools. *Social Studies, 6*, 14–19, 44–52, 122–125.

———. (1914b). The early teaching of history in secondary schools. *History Teacher's Magazine, 5*, 203–208.

Sabin, H. (1908). Is state uniformity of text-books desirable? *Journal of Education, 68*, 359–360.

Sanford, E. C. (1888). The relative legibility of the small letters. *American Journal of Psychology, 1*, 402–435.

Saveth, E. N. (1949). Good stocks and lesser breeds: The immigrant in American textbooks. *Commentary, 7*, 494–498.

———. (1952, February). What to do about "dangerous textbooks:" The pitfalls of pressure tactics. *Commentary*, 99–106.

Schenck, J. P. (1976). Sexism in textbooks: A guide to detection. *American Vocational Journal, 51*, 42–45.

Schlesinger, A. M. (1938). Introduction. In A Walworth, *School histories at war: A study of the treatment of our wars in the secondary school history books of the United States and in those of its former enemies* (xiii–xx). Cambridge, MA: Harvard University Press.

School text-books. (1915). *Outlook, 110*, 780–781.

Schools in Detroit reject Negro plea. (1962, November 24). *New York Times*, p. 10.

Schrag, P. (1967, January 21). The emasculated voice of the textbook. *Saturday Review, 50*, 74.

Schuyler, R. L. (1918). History and public opinion: The nationalist interpretation of history and Anglo-American antagonism. *Educational Review, 55*, 181–190.

Scott Foresman. (1972.) *Guidelines for improving the image of women in textbooks.* Glenview, IL: Author.

Scott, J. F. (1926). *The menace of nationalism in education.* London: Allen & Unwin.

Scott, M. G. (1916). One way to kill a goose which lays many golden eggs. *Typographical Journal, 49*, 455–456.

Searson, J. W. (1920). Limiting the spurious output of textbooks thru editing. *Proceedings of the National Education Association, 56*, 401–402.

Selke, B. E. (1983). U.S. history textbooks: Portraits of men and women? *Southwestern Journal of Social Education, 13*(1), 13–20.

Semple, E. C. (1903). *American history and its geographic conditions.* Boston: Houghton Mifflin.

Serl, E., & Pelo, W. J. (1919). *American ideals: Selected patriotic readings for seventh and eighth grades and junior high schools.* New York: Gregg.

Serviss, T. K. (1953). Freedom to learn: Censorship in learning materials. *Social Education, 17*, 65–70.

Sewall, G. T. (1987). *American history textbooks.* New York: Educational Excellence Network.

———. (1988). American history textbooks: Where do we go from here? *Phi Delta Kappan, 69*, 552–558.

Sewall, G. T., & Cannon, P. (1991). The new world of textbooks: Industry consolidation and its consequences. In P. G. Altbach, G. P. Kelley, H. G. Petrie, & L. Weis (Eds.), *Textbooks in American society: Politics, policy, and pedagogy* (pp. 61–70). Albany, NY: State University of New York Press.

Shawkey, M. P. (1918). The adoption of textbooks by state, county or district. *American Education, 21*, 402–404.

Sherwood, H. N. (1936). *Citizenship.* Indianapolis, IN: Bobbs-Merrill.

Shirer, H. S. (1919). Experiments in state publication. *Proceedings of the National Education Association, 57,* 465–468.

Simon, S. S., & Harmin, M. (1964). To study controversial issues is not enough. *Social Studies, 55,* 163–166.

Singer, H. (1975). The SEER technique. *Journal of Reading Behavior, 7,* 255–267.

Skoog, G. (1984). The coverage of evolution in high school biology textbooks published in the 1980s. *Science Education, 68,* 117–128.

Smith, K., Magee, E. B., & Seward, S. S. (1928). *English grammar: Correct and effective use.* Boston: Ginn.

Special New Republic report on book burning. (1953, June 29). *New Republic, 128,* 7–9.

Sprague, H. B. (1888). Discussion—State uniformity of textbooks. *Addresses and Proceedings of the National Education Association, 28,* 233–237.

Standing Committee on Textbooks (of the New England History Teachers' Association). (1898). Text-books in American history. *Educational Review, 18,* 480–502.

Steele, J. D. (1900). The teacher's aim. In G. Archibauld, *Joel Dorman Steele: Teacher and author* (pp. 68–85). New York: Barnes.

Stephens, H. M. (1916). Nationality and history. *American Historical Review, 21,* 225–236.

Stewart, C. E. (1964). Correcting the image of Negroes in textbooks. *Negro History Bulletin, 28* (2), 29–30, 42–44.

Stewart, M. S. (1950). *Prejudice in textbooks* (Public Affairs Pamphlet No. 160). New York: Public Affairs Committee.

Stewig, J., & Higgs, M. (1973). Girls grow up to be mommies: A study of sexism in children's literature. *Library Journal, 98,* 236–241.

Stillwell, C. (1950, September). America's schoolbook scandal. *Christian Herald,* 17–18, 68–70.

Stillwell, K. M. (1919). Making schoolbooks. *Elementary School Journal, 19,* 256–267.

Stormzand, M. J., & Lewis, R. H. (1935). *New methods in the social studies.* New York: Farrar & Rinehart.

Stuart, D. C. (1910, April 28). One way of making text books. *Nation, 96,* 428–29.

Survey of textbooks detects less bias against Blacks but little to please feminists. (1973, March 28). *New York Times,* p. 13.

Swett, J. (1888). The general function of the state in relation to school-books and appliances. *Addresses and Proceedings of the National Education Association, 28*, 198–201.

Swift, C. L. (1927, January). Featuring the humble textbook. *Journal of the National Education Association*, 11–12.

Taft, D. R. (1925). Textbooks and international differences. *Progressive Education, 2*, 92–96.

Tariff Bill's prohibition of revolutionary literature. (1929). *School and Society, 30*, 407–408.

Tarr, R. S., & McMurry, F. M. (1907). *A complete geography*. New York: Macmillan.

Tash, T. (1888). Free textbooks for free schools. *Addresses and Proceedings of the National Education Association, 28*, 220–225.

Texas may drop all textbooks for laptop. (1997, November 19). *New York Times*, p. 1311.

The textbook audit. (2000, April 21). *Salt Lake Tribune*, p. A22.

Text-book industry. (1918). *School and Society, 8*, 380–382.

Textbooks and the state. (1915, September 9). *Nation, 101*, 321–322.

Thomas, C. (1983). *Book burning*. Westchester, IL: Crossway.

Thomas, C. S. (1924). Educating the public to higher standards of textbook making. *Addresses and Proceedings of the National Education Association, 62*, 541–544.

Thompson, C. M. (1917). *History of the United States: Political, industrial, social*. Chicago: Sanborn.

Thorndike, E. L. (1921). *The teacher's word book*. New York: Teachers College Press.

Three types of textbook troubles. (1922). *School Review, 30*, 85–87.

Thursfield, R. E. (1947). Developing the ability to think reasonably. In R. E. Thursfield (Ed.), *The study and teaching of American history* (pp. 77–96). Washington, DC: National Council for the Social Studies.

Tidwell, C. J. (1928). *State control of textbooks, with special reference to Florida*. New York: Teachers College Press.

Tighe, C. B. (1920). The bias of history. *Historical Outlook, 11*, 139–140.

Todd, L. P., & Curti, M. (1961). *Rise of the American nation*. New York: Harcourt, Brace.

Townsend, E. J. (1891). The text-book question. *Education, 11*, 556–565.

Trecker, J. L. (1971). Women in U.S. history high school textbooks. *Social Education, 35*, 249–260, 268.

Tressler, J. C., & Shelmadine, M. (1940). *Building language skills.* Boston: Heath.

Trotter, S. (1906). *The geography of commerce: A textbook.* New York: Macmillan.

Turner, R. (1922). Are American school histories now too pro-British? *Landmark, 4*, 251–255.

Turner, R. C., & Dewey, J. A. (1973). Black history in selected American history textbooks. *Educational Leadership, 30*, 441–444.

Turpin, E. H. L. (1911). *A short history of the American people.* New York: Macmillan.

Tyson-Bernstein, H. (1989). Textbook development in the United States: How good ideas become bad textbooks. In J. P. Farrell & S. P. Heyneman (Eds.), *Textbooks in the developing world: Economic and education choices* (pp. 72–87). Washington, DC: World Bank.

UNESCO. (1959). *Primary school textbooks: Preparation-selection-use* (Pub. No. 204). Geneva, Switzerland: Author.

Van Cleef, E. (1937). *This business world: An economic and commercial geography.* Boston: Allyn & Bacon.

Vannest, C. G., & Smith, H. L. (1931). *Socialized history of the United States.* New York: Scribner's.

Vitz, P. C. (1986). *Censorship: Evidence of bias in our children's textbooks.* Ann Arbor, MI: Servant.

Vogel, M., & Washburne, C. (1928). An objective method of determining grade placement of children's reading material. *Elementary School Journal, 28*, 373–381.

Waite, R. W. (1972). How different are multiethnic urban primers? In S. G. Zinet (Ed.), *What children read in school: A critical analysis of primary reading textbooks* (pp. 71–78). New York: Grune & Stratton.

Walworth, A. (1938). *School histories at war: A study of the treatment of our wars in the secondary school history books of the United States and in those of its former enemies.* Cambridge, MA: Harvard University Press.

Wargny, F. O. (1963). The good life in modern readers. *Reading Teacher, 17*, 88–93.

Warren, D. M. (1868). *A new primary geography.* Philadelphia: Cowperthait.

Waterman, S. D. (1903). The advantages and disadvantages of a free text-book system. *Western Journal of Education, 8*, 362–366.

Weber, O. F. (1926). Methods used in the analysis of text-books. *School and Society, 24*, 678–684.

Webster, W. C. (1897). *Recent centralizing tendencies in state educational administration* (Studies in History, Economics, and Law, Vol. 8, No. 2). New York: Columbia University Press.

Wellington, E. E. (1929). Ridding the schools of propaganda. *Journal of the American Association of University Women, 22* (3), 157.

West, W. M. (1902). *Ancient history: To the death of Charlemagne* (Rev. ed.). Boston: Allyn & Bacon.

Whipple, G. (1964). Multicultural primers for today's children. *Education Digest, 29* (6), 26–29.

Whipple, G. M. (1929). The modern textbook and the school. *Journal of Education, 109*, 637–638.

———. (1930). The selection of textbooks. *American School Board Journal, 80* (5), 51–53.

Whitbeck, R. H. (1922). *High school geography.* New York: Macmillan.

White, W. (1939). Foreword. In National Association for the Advancement of Colored People. *Anti-Negro propaganda in school textbooks* (p. 3). New York: Author.

Wiik, S. L. (1973). The sexual bias of textbook literature. *English Journal, 62*, 224–229.

Wilder, H. B. (1937). Progress in social-studies textbooks. *Social Education, 1*, 313–318.

Williamson, J. H. (1979). Textbook publishing: Facts and myths. In J. Y. Cole & T. G. Sticht (Eds.), *The textbook in American society* (pp. 38–40). Washington, DC: Library of Congress.

Wilson, H. E. (1947). Intergroup relations in teaching materials. *Educational Record, 28*, 114–121.

Winship, A. E. (1908). State uniformity in text-books. *Journal of Education, 67*, 339–342.

———. (1909). The California text-book plan: Its history and results. *Journal of Education, 69*, 173–180.

———. (1915). Text-books—Educational, commercial and political. *Journal of Education, 81*, 285–288.

Wise, H. A. (1939). *Motion pictures as an aid in teaching American history.* New Haven, CT: Yale University Press.

Woodward, A. (1989). Learning by pictures: Comments on learning, literacy, and culture. *Social Education, 53*, 101–102.

Woody, C. (1920). Application of scientific method in evaluating the subject matter of spellers. *Journal of Educational Research, 1*, 119–128.

Wright, G. W. (1916). High school text books. *Sierra Education News, 12* (14), 83–85.

Zimmerman, R. (1975). Social studies textbooks still neglect racial minorities and women, and shortchange children. *Negro Educational Review, 26*, 116–123.

Zimmern, A. (1930, April). The League of Nations and the teaching of history. *New Era, 11*, 71–72.

Zinet, S. G. (1972). Values and attitudes in American primers. In S. G. Zinet (Ed.), *What children read in school: A critical analysis of primary reading textbooks* (pp. 87–97). New York: Grune & Stratton.

Zoll, R. (1999, September 12). More than 7 decades after "monkey trial," debate over teaching evolution unresolved. *Salt Lake Tribune*, pp. A1, A7.

Zook, G. F. (1939). International intellectual cooperation. *Educational Record, 20*, 508–535.

————. (1944). Foreword. In American Council on Education, *Latin America in school and college teaching materials* (Report of the Committee on the Study of Teaching Materials on Inter-American Subjects, pp. v–vi). Washington, DC: Author.

————. (1948). Foreword. In I. J. Quillen, *Textbook improvement and international understanding.* New York: American Council on Education.

AUTHOR INDEX

SUBJECT INDEX

THIS SERIES EXPLORES THE HISTORY OF SCHOOLS AND SCHOOLING in the United States and other countries. Books in this series examine the historical development of schools and educational processes, with special emphasis on issues of educational policy, curriculum and pedagogy, as well as issues relating to race, class, gender, and ethnicity. Special emphasis will be placed on the lessons to be learned from the past for contemporary educational reform and policy. Although the series will publish books related to education in the broadest societal and cultural context, it especially seeks books on the history of specific schools and on the lives of educational leaders and school founders.

For additional information about this series or for the submission of manuscripts, please contact the general editors:

Alan R. Sadovnik
Rutgers University-Newark
Education Dept.
155 Conklin Hall
175 University Avenue
Newark, NJ 07102

Susan F. Semel
The City College of New York, CUNY
138th Street and Convent Avenue
NAC 5/208
New York, NY 10031

To order other books in this series, please contact our Customer Service Department:

800-770-LANG (within the U.S.)
212-647-7706 (outside the U.S.)
212-647-7707 FAX

Or browse online by series at:

www.peterlangusa.com